THE UNCENSORED TRUTH:

LET'S TALK ABOUT SEX

by
L.G. Erikson

Divison House Publishing

The Uncensored Truth: Let's Talk About Sex

L.G. Erikson

ISBN 9780996115711

Acknowledgements

I would like to express my deepest gratitude to all the contributors that helped me to bring this idea to life as well as to everyone who shared their personal stories with me. Your contributions made my book much richer.

A special thank you to my editor Jack W. Peterson.

"No matter your age, every man's dream is in this book! Finally, I understand what most women are really thinking about and during sex. A great read at any age!"

— Jack Peterson
Author of the bestseller *"Balance of Power"* and *"A Thin Place"*

Table of Contents

Chapter 1:

INTRODUCTION

Many books have been written about sex. A lot of them attempt to explain to women what really turns him on. Some are very technical while others point out the so-called differences between men and women by suggesting ideas on how to deal with this lack of understanding the opposite gender.

This is NOT one of those books.

I came up with the idea when I finally realized that most women have never had real mind-blowing sex nor do they really know what it is. Initially targeted primarily towards women, I came to realize that men would likely benefit from the book's content as well because if women really take my message to heart, their relationship with their partner could easily turn into a gift that keeps on giving.

This book suits every kind of scenario: the one night stand, the casual dater, even the rock-solid traditional relationship. While it's mainly for heterosexuals, it might also benefit the lesbian community. Homosexuals express their sexuality much more freely in the first place, therefore they might not benefit as much from this book.

Many statements in this book are pretty straightforward, some might be perceived as blunt, nevertheless they're not meant to offend anyone. I made it a point not to oblige to political or social correctness simply because I believe that doing so often hinders people from telling the truth and ultimately it has become the root of many misunderstandings. Another reason why I wrote this book is that we tend to tiptoe around the subject of sex, which is the cause of a lot of confusion.

This book contains detailed descriptions of specific experiences from different people, all of which really happened.

I've written this book to change your perception of sex and, maybe in some form, of life.

Rule Number 1:

Open your mind.

This is where it all starts. Most women have all kinds of pre-conceived ideas. Some think sex is only there for procreation or to please their man. Some women may try to manipulate him into committing to them, providing them with goods; using sex as a negotiating tool, which inevitably finds some men becoming very good liars just to get laid, and the battle of the sexes began…

Then there is also the biological stuff; women are supposedly by nature not equipped to enjoy sex the way a man does due to how their brain is wired. They supposedly can't climax as easily as a man because of physical factors and everything is complicated by their emotions. They can't have sex without love – so they say – doctors, scientists, teachers, therapists and other worldly scholars.

What if I told you that any woman can have multiple orgasms, yes, even squirt (this is not only limited to porn stars), while enjoying the lust and the pure physicality of sex without the need to be emotionally involved? I'm not suggesting that sex is better if you're not emotionally involved, but only when we separate the two for the time being, we can weed out all these hindering ideas about sex. What if I told you that it's possible to melt with your sex partner without the need to be in love, but just for the simple enjoyment of the moment! Incredible sex is possible in and outside of relationships for both men *and* women.

You have to open your mind to new ideas, a different point of view. I'll show you how that's possible for any woman by sharing this knowledge that will give you a whole new kind of power, the kind of power you've always dreamed about. Use my information and knowledge any way you want. Whether you are just seeking a fantastic sex life, to hook him or to make him fall in love with you, or to have a much better relationship. Regardless of your motive, this is not a morality guide. It's simply a very different way to approach the subject of sex.

Chapter 2:

WHAT'S IN YOUR HEAD....

The mindset of how one approaches sex should not be an emotional issue. The mental process is most often the main factor in anything in life. One familiar issue is all the fears and worries many women often have such as "I'm too fat," or "Too unattractive," or other excuses as to why they can't have sex, such as "I don't feel like it....I'm in pain....I'm too tired....I'm bored....It's a sin....I'm only supposed to have sex to get pregnant....I'm too old....Sex is dirty....I never liked it before....I can't come," and whatever else you might come up with. None of these things have anything to do with the truth! They're just excuses.

Sex is supposed to be a pleasure treat and not some kind of chore one is supposed to do. If you ever had incredible sex you would never ever doubt that you as a woman are just as sexual as a man. Here's an important fact, the only difference I ever found: Men are just more willing to put up with bad or mediocre sex instead of none at all. The biggest mistake most women make with their approach to sex is to believe that they're just not as sexual as a man.

Yes, a man might think of sex much more often than many women but there are women with an incredibly strong sex drive as well. I can promise you, if you'll ever experience the incredibly high a sexual encounter can provide, your sex drive will raise... most likely far beyond anything you thought was possible.

Here's a good analogy: If I were to serve you mediocre food all day long, you would most likely still eat it simply because you need food to survive but your urge to eat it for mere pleasure would likely be relatively small, hence you probably wouldn't describe yourself as a foodie. On the other hand, if I served you something extremely delicious that makes your senses go nuts and tastes so good that you can't get enough of it, you'd probably be thinking of food much more frequently. It would make your mouth water and you would find yourself looking forward with excitement to the next delicious meal. Now, replace that train of thought with sex. It's as simple as that.

You can't have a craving for something that you never experienced!

How could you miss something if you never had it?

Pretty much all our likes and dislikes are created by a good or a bad experience. If something tasted shitty, most likely you wouldn't want to eat it again. The same principle applies to sex. If you've only had bad or mediocre sex, never had an orgasm or only by luck or chance, of course you won't think it's something you need to be happier. On the other hand, once you have had really good sex, it's a true game changer. You will never again perceive sex as a chore and I promise you the benefits are much broader than most of you may think.

Letting yourself drift off and submit to the adventure of mind-blowing sex is the very first step, and (this is a big one) BE SELFISH! I don't mean being selfish in the act, that you're only into being pleased, but in the sense that you want to get that high, where you won't settle for less, where you almost want to rip your man's skin off his flesh and, out of sheer lust, demand more and more!

Let me tell you, a man will never ever forget you, in his whole lifetime, if you totally opened up to him sexually, when you let all your inhibitions go and dive deep into the experience. A man will be forever hooked, even if that relationship won't last for other reasons. He will compare every other woman to you and miss what he had because it's so damn rare to find these kinds of women. I know because I've been there and I've heard it from a lot of men as well.

By the way, good sex has very little to do with whether you're physically perfect. In fact, that doesn't really matter. I'm not saying that it hurts, but if a pretty woman just lies there like a stick, it's like humping a blow-up doll.

You might be wondering what exactly I mean when I say you should dive deep into the experience by giving your all to him. That it's all about pleasing him or that you're supposed to do what whatever he wants?

No! A man is extremely turned on by a woman who's really into it, a woman who explodes or when he can make her completely insatiable. That's what *all* men want, no exceptions. I'm not talking about giving a performance as they do in porn I mean the real thing. It's something you can't fake, even though women are notoriously known for faking orgasms. By the way, some men do too. Great sex feels completely different if both partners are really into the sex they're having. If you ever had it, you would know what I mean (just the way you know what real love is once you've experienced it). I will tackle all the aspects of how and what you have to do to get there throughout this book.

Once a woman has the kind of sex I'm talking about, she will feel the same way about this particular guy, just as I described it earlier about men who find themselves hooked to a particular woman. Compared to the one she had that kind of mind-blowing sex with, anyone after him will fade until she knows how to re-create the same experience with a different partner. Once that happens, she'll discover something she didn't know about herself: women are *exactly the same* as men in that regard. Sex is a primal thing, deeply ingrained in our DNA. It is through implanting stereotypes into our mind, and social rules that women have forgotten what and who they truly are. If you ever had that kind of sex, you would never want to miss it, because it's as close as it gets to experiencing paradise here on earth. Mind-blowing sex is very addictive, but it's the best and healthiest addiction there is.

Sex is also very good for your health. Your aches, stress, fatigue, immune system and many diseases will benefit. You'll feel renewed, look amazing, and your mind will become much clearer as your senses become heightened and you'll have energy to sell. Most importantly, you'll feel more alive than you ever have. If there is any "heaven on earth," a hint of what paradise could feel like, this is the way to experience it!

Men *and* women are meant to have sex for the sake of having sex, not only to procreate.

Chapter 3:

LOVE VS. SEX

Being in love is without any doubt a beautiful thing. It makes you extremely happy, endorphins run wild, you want to hug the whole world and that's a great emotional mind frame to be in. It's one of those emotions that give you an incredible high. If that feeling is reciprocated, it's even better.

If the physical attraction is as strong as the emotional and you can melt the two into one, sex can be truly magical but even in very loving relationships sex eventually seems to become an issue. The main reason for that is the shift of emotions. That feeling of being in love gradually turns into "just" love. Often, once that first high is gone, people start to take in the environment more, things that didn't seem to matter beforehand, while you were in that "in love" mind frame. You'll also start to see the person you're with in a more realistic way (recognizing their flaws, for instance.) In that state, you find out if that person is a true match for you or not. I'm talking about the personality as well as sex. That's the time when people often start to take the other person for granted (since you're used to having them in your life), and things get a bit more complicated. Sexually you've tried it all, and it becomes a bit more of a mundane routine, and eventually, a certain level of boredom will set in.

By then, it is crucial to relight that spark, otherwise your relationship will become a very mediocre affair. Everything that made it something special once will go down the drain. Obviously there's much more to a relationship than sex, but make no mistake, it is the *one thing* that separates your romantic relationship from just being platonic friends. Many people with more life experience will tell you that this is just part of the process, that things change, and for that reason, it's important to be best friends, first and foremost. While that is important, it is a *big mistake* to base your relationship only on that. In many ways, it doesn't make any sense either. Why would you want to give up on that unique bond, solidified in a mind-blowing sexual connection and exchange it for being just friends and the occasional sex (because as a couple you're obligated to do so)?

Yes, there are immense challenges to keep a love affair going. Once you're used to each other, many distractions will come your way. On top of that, another big issue will surface: *Humans are not genetically equipped for monogamy* in the first place. Therefore, if your love life is not exciting anymore, temptations will definitely become a growing issue. For some, that might take a while, sometimes years, but eventually it's gonna happen. I'm not suggesting that monogamy isn't possible, but it is a choice, rather than something we're naturally programmed to be. So how do you prevent that from happening?

If I gave you a choice to pick between a mediocre relationship and one that is truly unique, where you both stand in opposite corners of a room, packed with people, and you feel your lover looking at you from afar with eyes filled with desire, anxiously waiting for the moment to finally rip your clothes off – which one would you pick?

If the two of you are a real match personality-wise and the love is strong on both sides, you can have that. The key is the kind of sex you're having. People don't drift apart or cheat as easily when they're completely sexually satisfied. I'm talking about the out-of-this world kind of sex, where the two of you are so connected that nothing else matters. This book will give you a lot insight in how to reach that.

The lack of good sex is the main reason – by far – why relationships fall apart. I'll elaborate on that in a later chapter much more in depth.

Chapter 4:

WHAT IS SEX?

In one sentence:

Everything is about sex.

Even in everyday situations, everything's about sex. Not literally, but people feel each others energy and that energy is tightly connected to sex. Only through sex did any of us come into existence.

Your sexual aura is a *huge* part of your being. How often does it happen that a person that isn't particularly attractive exudes some sort of unexplainable sexual vibe and is perceived as being very sexy and intriguing? While we don't know or can't explain such a phenomenon, some people present a very subtle vibe that is strongly connected to their sensuality and that is exactly what you feel when you meet them. It's not something you can pinpoint, but it's there.

People who have such an aura about them are often not even that aware of it, but if you would get to know them, you would likely find that there's something about them that is very sensual and that they are very open. Sex is all about senses. A sensual person is open to let their senses lead them, they have a certain vulnerability and they usually appear to be more in the moment and they carry a presence of being more alive.

In everyday life, when we encounter such a person with that sexual energy, we're immediately drawn to them. We pay attention to them. That doesn't mean you have to want to jump their bones, it's not really about that, it's more the fact that they draw you in, they get your attention because you perceive them as somewhat different than other people.

Of course that's beneficial because people with such personalities get noticed and paid attention to by their boss or find themselves being treated better by the salesperson in the store, the building manager, the mail man, the guy at the bank they try to get a loan from, anyone, fill in the blank. Again, it's not necessarily about you wanting to have sex with them, but they just have something inexplicable in their energy that automatically draws you in – whether it happens consciously or unconsciously. Often this is described as charisma, but it's really part of your basic make-up as a person. *It's the essence of you.*

All of this will make much more sense once you get the whole picture, better yet, hopefully by the end of this read, you'll be able to experience it yourself.

Sexual elements are much more obvious in advertisement, because almost everything is sold with an underlining sexual vibe whether a pretty model exudes it herself or the ad insinuates that you will become more irresistible if you buy that particular product. Look at any magazine, the sensuality of pictures, it's everywhere. Every celebrity is using sex to captivate the audience but it's not necessarily about much skin they show. We have become quite accustomed to seeing naked/ semi-naked people and yet, some exude that sexy vibe, while others just desperately try to get that image by stripping off all their clothes and still don't achieve a similar result. People can sense when others are "faking it," meaning it doesn't really come from their core.

Sexual energy is equal to life energy itself.

Chapter 5:

MEN VS. WOMEN

I have to touch on the psychological aspect a little bit to make my point:

We all know the age-old stereo types – men are hunters, women are prey.

There are all kinds of people who had an influence on you while you grew up, which created that stereotype in your head. Most likely, your point of view isn't really yours, but one that was implemented into your mind by your surroundings, people and the environment you grew up in.

Because we were brainwashed into believing in these stereotypes, both genders have established a certain behavior in order to attain a specific goal. Men often chase after women and perceive them as more valuable if they have to work harder to get them into the sack. Women tend to hold out, even if they really want to take a guy home, because they want to appear valuable. That by itself creates a subtext that, on a subconscious level, usually finds women placing much less value on their own pleasure when it comes to sex since she thinks she'll be less desired once she "gives it away." Meanwhile, it allows the man (as the hunter) to enjoy his victory psychologically.

Women who give into playing this game are usually very aware of that, the fact they may lose value once they sleep with a man. Consequently, they'll never let their sensual guard completely down to enjoy sex freely. And who can blame them? How can you freely enjoy something if it's part of a trade-off?

All learned stereo types create behaviors, and they in turn create labels.

Women are often called sluts when they sleep with anyone they like while men are considered cool and a hot stud when they sleep with every woman they can get. Society has taught us that sex is a tool and frequently finds women playing power games in order to become a more valuable trophy while encouraging men to turn into liars to become a successful trophy collector.

No one is born with such ideas. The environment has instilled them in our minds and unless we start to question them and weed them out, we will all end up living by rules based on society's labeling and not because we came to such conclusions on our own.

The human mind is so vulnerable to influences from outer sources that if one sells an idea long enough, eventually most people will buy into it. Something that started off as an idea eventually becomes a reality. In your mind, you won't question it anymore and accept it as a fact, even forget that it wasn't your idea in the first place. Brainwashing is a very powerful tool.

How do women use sex as a negotiating tool? There are many ways. "Marry me and you can have sex with me all the time,"...."Buy me that fur coat and I'll spread my legs,"...."Give me that job and I'll blow you." On the other hand, men will lie to beat women at this same game by faking an emotion (love) to get them to sleep with them. They've learned to buy women in many different ways just to get sex. A good example would be an old guy who has a young arm candy by his side, a girl/ woman that would never touch him if he didn't have all that wealth or connections.

Sex is a weapon in our society, a negotiating tool and whoever is more skillful in using it walks away a winner.

Unfortunately, it also takes the fun away.

It is also a big part of human nature to desire that unique something that is so hard to get. Imagine what happens when a man finds that particular woman. The one that makes him yearn for more and fulfills all his desires, the one that validates him, the one that shows him what a hot lover he is by making her so horny that she can't get enough of him.

Humans have an ego, how strong it is varies but we all have one. Everyone is flattered if they're made to feel special. A man who can make his lady go crazy sexually will be so flattered, he'll want to get that ego boost again and again. He will suddenly reach new orgasmic heights because of their merged energies. As mentioned before, I'm not suggesting that good sex is just about pleasing him, quite the contrary. However, unless he's had really good sex before that wasn't all about him he might not know that about himself. Oftentimes men don't know good sex either. The only difference between men and women is that men are taught that they are the more sexual creature. The fact that he wakes up with a boner makes his sexual nature more apparent. Many women have sexual dreams at night. They're just not as aware of it because they don't wake up with their crotch on fire. Mind-blowing sex is about merging the two sexual energies and making it temporarily one (which might or might not to be in conjunction with love).

But now, let's get to the famous exception from the rule: A few women always seem to have such an easy game that they almost never get cheated on (very few might cheat but certainly not because of sexual boredom). They can not only get pretty much every guy, they usually keep him hooked, even after they're not together anymore. He will still dwell in his memories and chances are he'll never find that again with any other woman. This applies to all kinds of men; the player, the hot stud, the desired and the not so desired.... the average Joe. I've seen this happen to the kind of guys girls are drooling over just as much as to an average type.

This woman (the "man eater" type) I described earlier can be beautiful, pretty or just somewhat attractive but she's undoubtedly a sexual treasure and most definitely has the sexual aura I described earlier. These are the kinds of women that can turn a player into a clingy pussycat, even into someone who wants to commit. (This has to do with the yin/ yang effect; I'll get into this in a later chapter.)

This is just an example of how the tables can turn if the circumstances are different. I'm most definitely not an advocate for trapping men with sex into a commitment. My sole purpose of writing this book is to open your eyes about the nature of sex, so you can enjoy it too.

Give someone a taste of paradise and they'll keep coming back for more. Sex is very, very, very different when both really dive into it.

Chapter 6:

THE MIRACLE CURE

Before I get into the juicy details of mind-blowing sex, I must briefly review the health aspect of it because really good sex has tremendous health benefits.

First of all, your energy level increases drastically. The same applies to physical strength and your immune system. Aches and pains of any sorts will get much better, you may find that you can deal much better with stress. Your mood will improve, you'll be able to focus better and you'll develop a stamina that is nothing short of amazing.

Mentally, the best way to describe the above is that it's like coming home to the real you. I can promise you that you'll never feel better. The French have an expression, "le petit mort." It means "a little bit of death" in regards to an orgasm. Whoever invented that phrase knew what mind-blowing sex is. This kind of orgasm feels a bit like drifting off into the stratosphere. When you come back to earth, it leaves you with the feeling that if you were to die right now it would be alright. It's the ultimate high, the ultimate way to feel alive and a much better high than any drug could possibly provide you with.

The more you experience this kind of sex the better it will get. It's also the ultimate rejuvenator. You want to stay young, mentally and physically? This is the answer. The body is nothing short of a miracle when it comes to curing ailments and restoring a youthful appearance if it's provided with the right tools. The best part is that it's not only free but so much fun! People with this kind of sex life live longer, are much happier, and less depressed.

The body needs and craves sex.

If sex was only to procreate, women would only get horny when they're ovulating, and men would only pick up sexual vibes when women are fertile. Put aside past experiences, all your religious and social restrictions and whatever else there is that made you believe that sex isn't important for your well-being and that sex is mainly there for procreation.

Sex is like a super-food for the body. While you can live without it, it will enhance your body and longevity tremendously.

Chapter 7:

KNOW YOUR BODY

Of course it helps a lot when you know your body well, what it's turned on by. If it is vaginal sex or oral sex, which part of your vagina is most sensitive? Is it the inner side or one particular side of your labia, the clit, or the g-spot? Is it your anus? Do you like it rougher or softer, or a combination of the two?

Without turning this into a technical book, I do recommend to masturbate to figure out what it is that you're into, if you're not entirely sure. This whole book is about opening your mind. Try a vibrator, especially the one called the rabbit (mans gift to female anatomy), and explore a little.

See if you can make yourself come, and keep going, and try again, and see how far you can take it. Can you have multiple orgasms, can you squirt? Squirting can be reached when you feel that deep inner built up, an orgasm that comes from the depth of your loins, when your labia starts swelling up and you feel an orgasm building. Once the contraction moment is there, most women think, "Oh, this was the orgasm," and stop. Big mistake! That's when you have to keep stimulating. You will reach a point where you'll feel like you'll lose your mind, almost like you need to pee at the same time (and sometimes that can actually happen too, no need to panic). That's when you have to keep stimulating that spot that makes you so horny. If you can manage to keep the stimulation going, you will come to that point where your body just keeps trembling in lust, where you want to come again, and again, and again, like a recurring wave, and eventually an ejaculate will come out, almost like a sperm, only that it isn't sperm... welcome to female ejaculate, sister, you just squirted!

Part of incredible sex is obviously recognizing what works for you. The right lover might help you discover it, but it's important that *you* know your body well. What if you never come across someone who will open that sexual floodgate? My goal is to get you there on your own! However, once you experience the kind of amazing sex I'm talking about with a person, whether it's through their help or *your* own initiation, masturbating will pale in comparison.

Another valuable self-discovery tool: watch porn! Before you think I've lost it, I do have a very good reason for the suggestion. Most people have various mental blocks when it comes to experimenting or trying something new. Maybe you've never had a lover that tried a lot of different positions or used toys or played out different scenarios with you or they hurt you physically (clumsy in bed or selfish) and that's why you didn't like a certain thing. All of that has an impact on how you see yourself sexually.

The reason why I suggest watching porn (by yourself, that is!) is to find out what turns you on. We all know that porn is (bad) acting but you still see people having sex in different scenarios. You see men and women playing with toys or having group sex. You will see different body types, people of different ages and various skin tones. Some will act more submissive, some will moan very passionately, while others do a lot of dirty talk. Some of them will show more visual stimulation, or they focus more on touching. You will see them in different settings, indoors, outdoors, being watched, being dressed in certain outfits, or plain naked. They may be soft or rough with each other, slower or faster, using all kinds of positions while doing oral, vaginal, anal.... the list is endless. When you watch porn by yourself, there's no judgment. You can privately observe your favorite scenes....the ones that make you wet, or make you fantasize. Just watch with an open mind and don't censor yourself. There might be things that turn you on that you didn't expect. If that happens, don't judge yourself, as there's no reason to feel guilty, that's why you're supposed to watch it alone. This is all about discovering what triggers your interest, and even if it's something more exotic, that's all fine. This is definitely a way to find yourself sexually.

You might have a certain image in your head about how you perceive your sexual identity but in time, you might find out that what truly turns you on or off is something entirely different than what you expected. Either way, you will learn a lot about yourself.

One more very important thing: Make peace with your physical image! If you're blessed with a beautiful body or you place a lot of value on your looks and you work hard to keep your body in perfect shape you might not have a problem looking at yourself naked in the mirror. (Even though some of the most critical people are often those in perfect shape.) Fact is that most people don't fit into this category. You could be average or overweight, skinny-boney or full-figured, it doesn't really matter. It's very important that you accept your body. I'm not saying you have to be in love with your image but you must come to terms with your looks. First of all, no one is perfect;

secondly, once people get it on they perceive almost everything as more perfect than it is. Guys often become overwhelmed when they have sex. If you were the sneaky type of woman and you were to try to manipulate someone into marrying you, a guy would probably say "I do," while he's inside of you, just because he's so into you in that moment. This is *not* meant as an insult to women and I'm not suggesting that women need to manipulate a guy into marrying them with sex. I just want to demonstrate what a man's mind frame is when he's aroused. The last thing he'll think about is your looks. Plus, how many men are perfect?

On the contrary, if you're beautiful, but a bore in bed, they'll remember that as well. There is an expression about that and it's pretty much on point: "Show me a beautiful woman, and I'll show you a guy who's tired of fucking her." Great looks might get the girl the boy for the moment, but to hold on to him she needs to be much more than just pretty. Sex is way less about looks than people think. The aforementioned expression is also meant to say that a guy will leave a pretty girl just as easily as a not so pretty girl if he's tired of her.

In reverse (just so you don't think I only accuse women of being boring in bed), a woman might tolerate a male bore as a partner much longer due to the misconception that sex is not supposed to mean so much to a woman. However, should she find someone who pays more attention to her, who might appear to be a potentially better lover, she will cheat on her man for the same reasons.

I can guarantee you that women turn into very sexual people once they've had the kind of sex I'm hinting at (so far.)

Chapter 8:

SEX AND RELATIONSHIPS

As I mentioned earlier, humans are not naturally equipped with a monogamy gene. It's a choice! Sexual boredom is and always will be the main reason why people cheat and leave each other. They might not admit it because our society has become so concerned about being politically correct that people have become very good when it comes to lying to each other and, worse yet, lying to themselves. Many have become such good liars when it relates to social issues that they fool themselves into believing their own lies.

Ask yourself a simple question: Why are you in a romantic relationship? What is the difference between a good friendship and a romantic relationship? SEX! Let's just cut out the "friends with benefits" situation for a moment here. I will address that unique concept in a moment.

Ideally, you can talk to your close friends about your problems, your innermost worries and hardships, but for one reason or another, you're not attracted to each other sexually.

Then you find your partner in crime, the one you want to share your life with. Let's assume for a moment that the sex was at least somewhat good at the beginning, due to the endorphins people in love release in their brains that create that kind of enchantment. Eventually endorphins wear off, and it turns from being in love into "just" love. At some point (how long that takes will vary) after you've done everything sexually, you know each other inside out and sex usually becomes a bit more mundane. Eventually every other problem you might have had with each other or certain things that might not have bothered you about your partner before becomes amplified. All of a sudden you dislike your partner's way of chewing, the way he sleeps, how moody he is, how sloppy, how he handles money, how he avoids confrontations, how aggressive he can be, or how he would rather watch football than spend time with you. However small or big the issue is it will become more significant and bothersome once the sex is not that exciting anymore.

Of course, as a living breathing human being, our emotions (love) can change throughout the years but let's not forget that our minds can be so easily manipulated.

Let me demonstrate with a small exercise what exactly that means. Try this for a moment: think of the worst thing that's ever happened to you, try to remember every little detail and I promise you that you will feel the same way now as you felt back then. Same goes for the best thing that's ever happened to you. This proves clearly that how you feel, and how you perceive things, is heavily impacted by your mind, and what exactly you focus on. A bad emotion from the past can drag you down in the present the same way it did when it happened originally whereas a positive emotion from the past can make you feel as good now as it did back then. Therefore, if you allow yourself to drift off and dwell on the negative aspects of a person, you will only pay attention to these bad traits. Add to that the fact that you sleep with each other way less and it becomes a recipe for disaster.

Now imagine having a phenomenal sex life instead. Even many years later it is still thrilling. You may be having some problems (such as the loss of your job, unexpected expenses) but you still share that exciting bond of sexual heaven with your partner. It will strengthen your union, make you more resilient towards illnesses and stress and you're much better equipped with dealing with your problems. Not only that, it makes you much happier and more balanced when you're still intimately connected in a very exciting way. That by itself is a bond that is much harder to break than someone's who's not only dealing with issues but also with sexual frustrations.

Now, let's touch briefly on the cheating factor (more in-depth later). People might cheat for ego boosts, feeling alone, being apart for a long time or perhaps repetitive fighting but definitely it is most often because they need a thrill in bed because sex has become a chore, something mechanical. Often they won't admit to it because it's a no-no, a social taboo that one is not supposed to say.

Due to human nature, it's almost impossible to assume that one will never cheat no matter what but I can assure you that people who still have mind-blowing sex after many years have a much better chance on staying faithful. If you have the kind of sex that everyone only dreams of, why would you run off to look for someone else? Chances are you won't get the same thing.

To prove my point: I know a couple that has an incredible sex life and, after many fights, they both ran off to sleep with someone else only to return to each other because their flings were disappointing.

Friends with benefits:

I'm giving this its own category because there is a whole psychology aspect attached to it that most people don't consider. What exactly does it mean to have a "friend with benefits?" In plain, blunt words it means that you're attracted to each other physically but for one reason or another, you don't really like to be with them. One reason could be that you don't like each other's personality as a partner but do as a friend. Another reason might be that one of or both of you think you can find someone better suited to your tastes. Ultimately, it means that you/they just don't want to go out and find a new person every time they want to fuck. It's a convenience.

I personally think that this is not the best concept. I believe it's much easier to take home a stranger and then part ways because it's much less confusing but…. for some people it works. You just have to make sure that both parties know exactly what the situation is and understand that all they want is a regular person to have sex with….nothing more or less. However, there is always the possibility that it *can* turn into more, especially if they have mind-blowing sex. The reason is simple….they're friends. It's not as cut and dry emotionally if you're really hooked on to a person sexually because as friends you usually hang out with each other. But DO NOT count on this! If you know you have feelings for this person and you give into sex with the hopes that it might turn into more, you're setting yourself up for a possible disappointment. Don't speculate that he might change his mind. It goes without saying that it could be the other way around as well. Guys also have female friends that they might like more than they're willing to admit, and they see an intimate involvement as a chance to change the relationship, all the more because women are supposed to be so emotional. Remember the character Scarlett Johansson portrayed in the movie *"He's Just Not That Into You"?* While mind-blowing sex can change the perception of people in terms of how they feel about each other, it doesn't have to. There's always a chance that it's just a very beautiful experience, which doesn't devaluate the act itself at all. Yes, mind-blowing sex can hook two people together but if one or both of them still feel that they would be bad life partners, they might still reason their way out of it, albeit having a hard time to replace what they found sexually.

This is why this concept can get very confusing for people. I don't want to point my reader in a direction in terms of choosing what they should or shouldn't do morality-wise but, in this case, consider yourself warned. This situation is hard to compartmentalize because if you have sex and stay with them that night it might feel like a relationship rather than a hookup, because you're friends. If you leave right away one of you might feel insulted and "used" because you're also friends. In many ways, it's a pretty slippery slope. I know quite a few people who's "friends with benefits" situation turned into a big mess. Therefore, if you must, do it with your eyes wide open. Make sure you know exactly what you're agreeing to, talk about it openly and *don't fool yourself* with false hopes. Don't make any assumptions. If it changes the relationship (feelings develop from one or both ends), you will feel it and then it's definitely time to talk about it.

Hookups:

Hookups can work for men *and* women. The key is the mind frame. Let's say you're in a lounge, dancing with your friends.

All of a sudden, you meet a guy. He's from out of town, just visiting. You start dancing together and an undeniable chemistry evolves. The conservative part of you might tell you that it's slutty behavior to go home with a stranger. But then again, there is the chemistry and an opportunity to explore another human being that won't be around for long. To make this easy, let's say you're single. If you're into the guy and he's into you, why not explore this unique situation. You both found each other and there's something there. Most people don't have chemistry with others on a daily basis, so in many ways you can see it as a gift. As long as both of you know what it is, that it's a onetime thing, and you're clear on that in your head and you don't make it more than it is in your mind, you can have a great experience. You might have learned that you're supposed to "save your body for the right one," but what if there's no "right one" in sight? Why can't you take advantage of the opportunity presented?

Let me make another thing also very clear: If both know what it is, it has very little to do with "using someone." If both of you get pleasure out of a one-night-stand, then how can this be wrong or called "he's using you?" If anything, you'd be "using each other." All these pre-conceived ideas pretty much insinuate that a guy has pleasure when having sex while the woman is not. Otherwise, there wouldn't be a reason to call it "using someone." There's nothing wrong with pleasurable consensual sex. As long as you don't pretend that it's anything else but taking advantage of the moment, no one will get emotionally involved. It's in your head, that's where you decide whether "to go there" emotionally or not.

One thing you shouldn't do is have them sleep over or stay at their house. Nice guys who do hookups sometimes think it's the nicer thing to do, to stay. But often it just creates an awkward moment in the morning (plus it's more confusing if you play "boyfriend and girlfriend" for a night). If it's just a hookup, it's not about love so why pretend and cuddle up to someone who you're not in love with?

Multiple hookups with the same person:

I call this being lovers. Let's say the aforementioned hookup is not someone from out of town. You met, you felt attracted to each other; you went home together and the sex was good for both and you want a repeat. If you end up meeting again, having sex repeatedly, it's pretty obvious that there is a lot of chemistry. If you don't talk about anything too revealing and personal, he could just turn into a steady lover. However, should the two of you decide to get to know each other, there is still a lot of potential that it could turn into more, since the chemistry factor is already there.

Sex with the Ex:

This is often done to dwell in the past, meaning you haven't found someone better to sleep with and it brings you back to the ex. Or he initiated it. Guys often do that, and since they've practiced being emotionally unattached their whole lives (I'm referring to the aforementioned stereotypes).That's why they're much better at it than women. Some women, especially the ones who believe that they can't have sex without being emotionally attached, do it because they want to rekindle the relationship, often against their better judgment. While I'm not inclined to give relationship advice in this book, I do want to mention that it takes effort to really change. I'm referring to the issues you had, the ones that broke it off in the first place. Often people live in a make-belief world where they see things *the way they want to see them*, rather than seeing things the way they really are. While it's possible that people change, in reality they often don't (at least not easily or in a big way). Ultimately, this scenario is somewhat similar to the "friends with benefits" category. If both of you are on the same page, meaning you do it solely for sexual pleasure, no one will get hurt. The benefit is that you definitely know each other well.

Chapter 9:

"NORMAL SEX" VS. MIND-BLOWING SEX

It's always tricky to use the word "normal" to describe something since it's a term created by society and it can mean very different things in different cultures and social settings. So let me elaborate:

When I use the phrase "normal sex," I mean anything, ranging from the average "I'm gonna hop on top of you and hump you until I come," (male) to "I'm glad that's over," (woman). Or "hopefully we got pregnant now," (mainly women), "Ok, that was alright," (man or woman), or "how long do I have to blow you until you come," (woman or man.... just replace the latter with 'eat you' instead of 'blow you' for the man). Others could be "maybe in time it'll be more fun" (either one), and "why does he always finish before I'm ready?" (woman)... and the list goes on.

To be very clear:

I'm *not* insinuating that the sex positions/lack of acrobatics are the problem.

What I mean is the way you *involve yourself* in the act. You can have completely traditional sex and it can blow your mind.

Sex acrobatics have nothing to do with it. It's the enjoyment factor, how turned on you are. This is a book about breaking through limitations and dropping judgmental behavior.

However, even when sex is fairly exciting for both parties, there's often that subtle feeling that it could be better, that it was better in your head (as a fantasy, which men as well as women have but often don't admit to) than in reality or that something was missing or your sex partner didn't quite get what you wanted, and similar things. On a side note, while it is very normal to have fantasies about sex or other partners, if you have truly mind-blowing sex this won't even occur to you while in the act. That's also a good indicator that the sex you're having right now – while in your mind you're having sex with the hot neighbor – can't be that hot after all.

Getting back to the point that somehow this was a tad better in your mind than in reality, therefore you must face an important fact: you had half-ass sex, you both didn't allow yourself to "melt into each other." Both parties are guilty of that.

But what exactly do I mean when I use the term "melt into each other"?

Often that happens by accident the first time, which is why most people don't understand what it is. They think it's a onetime thing, some special sexual connection they have with that one particular person. They often don't understand that it was the connecting part with the other person, that they allowed themselves to really open up to them. I'm not suggesting that you can create that with everyone, obviously chemistry is always the key, but don't confuse sexual chemistry with being in love. Any time you have chemistry with someone, you have the potential for mind-blowing sex.

I will tell you a few stories to give you an example of mind-blowing sex, so you get an idea what it feels like. The first story took place during a casual hookup, turned into a lover's situation, the second one in a relationship:

Story Number 1: The Initiator

They meet at work. He was the kind of guy who could have any woman. He is extremely handsome, charismatic, smart, witty, creative, and very, very sexy. Every woman has her eye on him. They start talking, flirting, and over a course of four, five months, a strong sexual tension builds up. Finally, they spontaneously decide to meet up at night in a bar. From the very beginning it's obvious they will go home together.

After flirting up a storm in several bars, he kisses her. The kind of hot kiss you see in porn, where they start off with a very deep tongue kiss, sucking each other's lips, slowing down for a second, only to really tongue each other harder. After the passionate kissing episode, they go to another bar, where the tension builds up even more and eventually they go to her place.

It became obvious that he had a lot of experience (in fact, she later found out that he'd been in a couple of porn movies). They tore each other's clothes off; he sucked her breasts, put his fingers into her vagina, and then made her kneel on the couch with her ass turned towards him. He went down on her, licking her vagina and butthole from behind. When he finally fucked her on the couch, they came at the same time, and both had a very strong orgasm.

A bit later, they had traditional sex in various positions in different spots of the apartment.... on the floor, on the bed, he on top, she on top, from behind and sideways, before switching to anal in every position one can imagine. He was a very good dirty talker, using the kind of language that was very graphic yet very sensual. From the beginning, when he fucked her on the couch, she was able to just drift off into the experience and, while he couldn't see her face, he could feel her completely opening up to him which made his orgasm much more intense as well.

Throughout the night, their sexual connection grew even more intense, their energies becoming one as they kept exploring. While it had the feel of live porn it was so much more than that. They connected in a spiritual level, where both core energies became one and they could feel the others lust build up. They took each other's energy and shared it with each other, the kind that makes you so horny that you want to rip the others skin off (figuratively speaking, of course). They eventually experienced the core of their being and melted into one. Both experienced it the same way. After a while, he said to her, "Wow, I've had a lot of good sex, but never like this."

Now, why did it happen there? And how did it happen? Call it a lucky coincidence. They had an incredible chemistry, he had a good hand in doing the right things to her and she just got carried away. When she experienced her first multiple orgasm, he was hooked.

Throughout the next two years, they kept coming back to each other to relive that experience again and again. Eventually, they had a huge falling out and didn't talk to each other for about four years. When he finally contacted her again, they met and talked. He confessed that he didn't have sex for almost two years afterwards because the whole experience was so unique that it had shaken him to the core. She took a long sexual break as well, instinctively knowing that this is not something you can easily replace. For the first six months she dreamed of it, every time she saw something remotely sexual, she saw him in her mind. For a long time, she too didn't want to sleep with someone else.

The two never had a serious relationship. They were just lovers that experienced this mind-blowing sex from the very first time on. While they got along and shared many common interests, they realized that their personalities just didn't match.

Throughout their time together they were both eager to bring each other to a state of ecstasy and drifted off into the experience, allowing each other to really see the other's true nature. It was all the way to the core with no holding back, no inhibitions, a complete dropping of their guards. That's the reason why it was so different. Yet, they were never in a relationship. This is a very good example that this kind of connection can develop right away if both open their mind to it.

At the time, she assumed that it's a onetime situation, that she might never find that again…. however, it did happen, when she least expected it.

Story Number 2: The surprise encounter

Guy meets girl, guy really likes the girl, but the girl only likes him to a certain degree. She's by no means into him. In the past, when she fell for someone, it was an immediate feeling, something exhilarating and thrilling that drew her towards a guy. This one was different. He was very average at first blush, and not really her type either.

Out of boredom, she agrees to exchange numbers and they go on a date. When she meets him for their date, she's even less impressed with his physicality and the things he says. He even strikes her a bit as an oddball when they talked in the car on their way to an art show, where she would meet his friends. After having a surprisingly fun date, he drives her back to her house, uses the "I have to pee" excuse to get access to her place. After relieving himself, he forces his move. Initially, she's a bit reluctant since she wasn't really attracted to him but gives into his kiss which is very gentle and sensual. They get aroused and have sex. To her surprise, it was pretty good and he leaves. Since he caught her by surprise with this experience, she decides to give him another shot. When they go out again on the following weekend, they end up at his friend's barbecue which is close to his apartment.

Since she didn't have her car, she knew she was temporarily stuck with him and, since the sex was somewhat good the first time, she decides to give it another go. He was a very gentle, sensual, and slow kisser unlike the other thrilling experience she's had with the other guy. This time it was progressing very slowly, almost tantric. He's kissing her everywhere, goes down on her, and really pays attention to how she responds, what makes it better for her (tongue technique, speed, pressure, sucking the clit), and she proceeds to get really turned on to a near orgasmic state. She decides to return the favor and blows him. They do that for a while before moving to the bedroom.

He gets on top of her and gently starts fucking her. He's a bit on the larger side so she can really feel him inside, and since he starts off very slowly, she feels really good. Throughout the whole time, he makes eye contact with her, and she takes it all in. An intimacy develops that she didn't expect.

Then he unexpectedly pulls out to take a break but also tells her that he can easily go on for a long time. After a few minutes, they start touching each other again, and this time she climbs on top of him, slowly gliding up and down on his penis, kind of like giving him a lap dance in the horizontal position. They both are turned on very quickly and she pushes him down and starts rubbing her vagina with his penis....up and down, up and down. Moments later, he makes her sit on his face and starts eating her again and looks at her while doing it. They keep eye contact as she suddenly feels an orgasm coming up deep from her core like a wave that keeps on growing stronger and stronger. She can sense that her orgasm will be much more intense than what she normally experiences. It keeps building. Suddenly he stops for a split second, looks at her for a brief moment before continuing. She starts to tremble, moving her pelvis, directing the speed, his movement, while moving her hips in a circular motion. Within seconds, she feels the orgasm coming but in a way that is so unbelievably deep, she has to close her eyes. Then she stares deeply into his eyes while he's deeply hooked into her gaze and she's starts rubbing herself all over his mouth and, finally, explodes onto him. She can feel that deep pull, almost like an out-of-body experience as her heart races. Her blood pressure escalates as an unbelievable energy rises inside of her. Her man is totally sunken into the experience. She starts shaking, almost out of control, then her orgasm explodes, over and over again while their eyes are remain hooked into each other as if each were looking into the others soul. After multiple orgasms, she finally squirts onto his face. It's almost like a small near death experience. After a very long pause, she finally slides off him, only to pick it up again minutes later. This time she blows him.

When it's clear he's almost ready to come, he takes her sideways and then she slides on top. Within minutes, he comes inside of her.

After a very short break, they begin again. He takes her from behind, but in a very gentle way. When he switches to anal, she's reluctant. He pushes her down flat on her stomach with her legs together and penetrates her. (By the way, this is the most effective and painless way to have anal sex. If either of them touches her on her clit while being penetrated anally, she can get pleasure out of this, too, no matter how big the guy is and no matter how tight the girl's butt is.) They almost come simultaneously, stop right before, and take another break.

About 20 Minutes later they start again, this time with the missionary position. He flips her on top and she begins rubbing her clit on his penis. Once again, she is extremely turned on. Then, he surprises her. He asks her to pee on him....something she had never done before. She was asked to do so in the past, but could never bring herself to do it. He's very patient, explaining to her why he likes it, how it feels to him – like a very soft shower, hence the term golden shower. She tries for a while but can't bring herself to do it.

A bit later, they try again. This time, she can do it a little bit. In time she learns that it's about letting go mentally, let it all just flow. (By the way, if one can do it while having an orgasm, it's pretty incredible.) Moments later, he comes really hard. They take another break.

After a little rest, they take a shower together, and for the first time, there is a lot of light so they can see each other. While he is gently washing her hair, she turns to face him. They start touching each other's genitals. Their eyes are hooked on each other and their souls become one for a moment. Suddenly, she can sense the whole "him," and he senses all of her. They touch each other gently while looking at each other. They both come simultaneously just by touching each other.

They have sex all night and again the next day and the next night followed by another day, and another night. Then he drives her home.

In the following weeks the sex gets more intense with every moment. They experience extreme highs together and can't get enough of each other. They explore everything together, even things they both perceived as a taboo before like drinking each other's pee, and licking eating each other's anus. Golden showers become part of the game. Every time they're together, it's the same. They can't leave their hands off each other, they're not able to sleep for more than maybe a few hours, and have sex in record numbers.

Mind you, neither of them was into "exotic" sex practices with anyone else beforehand. They just started exploring with each other and events just took a natural flow. The more they gave into each other, the more intense the sex and their orgasms became. If they could talk to you now, they would tell you that this was not only the best sex they ever had up to this point in their lives; they had taken sex to a whole new level. They were addicted to each other. Sex was out of this world, they barely needed any sleep and were healthy, resistant to colds and whatever else was going around, and looked incredibly good. So good in fact, that some of her friends asked her what she had "done" to herself.

I should also mention that they had a three year relationship and the sex never became mundane, despite having sex all the time. The relationship fell apart for other reasons.

To make this very clear, this is not some extraordinary woman. In fact, she too, had many misconceptions about her sexual identity, just as many other women. In fact, after she broke up with her very first boyfriend as a 17 year old, she thought she'd never enjoy sex with anyone else, or love someone else, when in reality it wasn't really love or good sex in the first place. It's not that she didn't like sex but she had also had faked orgasms before, made excuses to avoid sex with a boyfriend, or wondered when it's gonna be over, never tried anything super-kinky before and did all the common things women do in the bedroom. She was just like any other ordinary woman, until these two experiences took place.

After the second experience, she realized that one can recreate this kind of sex with different people and now she experiences sex in general very differently. She's become insatiable; she's extremely sexual and really enjoys it, in and outside of relationships.

All it takes is one time, that one person who manages to open up that barrier inside of you that will make you truly explore and let it all go and allow yourself to fully experience your true nature. It's like stepping into a world of magic.

Once you've experienced this kind of sex, you'll never want to miss it. Then you understand what sex can be. Anyone can get there, but you don't have to leave it up to chance, to maybe (maybe never) get together with someone who will get you out of your shell. *You* can be the initiator.

By the way, both guys from the stories (and as you saw, they're very different types and the relationships were very different as well) said that they never experienced anything like this before and ever since. Both couldn't get the girl out of their head and compared any other girl to her because this kind of sex is extremely rare. Not because this is a special breed of women, she was just like everybody else. Most women just never encounter a guy that can get that part of them to open up. In many ways, she was very lucky that it happened to her. Fact is that any woman can have that. So why not be the initiator? If you start it off the right way, your next sexual encounter can be very different.

Chapter 10:

THE ACT OF MIND-BLOWING SEX

In one sentence:

When people have "normal" sex, they're in their own world during the act; when people have mind-blowing sex it's about *merging these two worlds into one.*

How YOU can create mind-blowing sex:

It doesn't matter if you're in a relationship or if it's a casual hookup, the only difference is that you know your boyfriend/husband better sexually. Sometimes it's harder to change established patterns in a relationship, since the two involved have gotten to know each other a certain way and became accustomed to it.

So in a relationship, the next time you want to have sex, start it off with a light and easy setting, like going out for dinner and – I can't stress this enough! – flirt with your partner. Imagine you see him for the first time, take everything in about his looks, his personality… Then you see him already in a slightly different light. It's very important to break old accustomed habits. Have a drink or two. Look sexy, dress the part! Not overdone, men often get turned off by that, but since it's your partner, you should know what works for him.

If the vibe in the air is a slightly different one, one of flirtatious behavior, he's gonna register that already as a different signal. Laughing, smiling is something that turns on every guy.

Have a few drinks but not too many, same goes for him. Certain kinds of alcohol kill a guy's ability to perform, so don't let him get drunk. You want the vibe to be sexy, light and easy with a slightly different energy between the two of you.

Once you start to get it on, it's VERY IMPORTANT to keep eye contact. Men generally like to take things in visually, but women also get visually stimulated. The reason why they tend to think that they're not so visual is because they are often too much in their heads ("do I look good, will he look at my belly, can he see that pimple on my back," and whatnot). Once you push that sexual reset button (where you don't allow yourself to get carried away by judgmental thoughts), this might be something you perceive very differently. If you look at your naked bodies, how he's going down on you, or at him, while you're going down on him, and you do it solely from the point of view to take each other in and share the pleasure with eye contact, this will change. You will be turned on by the visual as well. Look at the beauty of the sexual dance, rather than focusing on your flaws. Your attention will go to whatever you focus on.

Do things sensually, like taking off your clothes, make sure he's watching you. Even if you're not the type that would strip for your guy with sexy moves, you can still do this slow and conscious and with pleasure, so he pays attention to you. It's not so much about giving him a show; it's more about enjoying what you're doing and sharing that with him. He needs to see you and the situation in a different light and YOU need to see the whole act of sex in a different light as well!

I'm not gonna tell you what kind of sex you're supposed to have (foreplay, oral, positions or how much time to take with what, that's all very subjective stuff), because that wouldn't make sense. You can do things you've done before, but do them sensual. Whether you go down on him, or he does it to you, make sure you look at each other, look at your bodies, and take it all in. Guys LOVE to watch; ALL OF THEM – no exception. If you can connect with him there, you're already on the right track. Don't climb under the sheets; don't have sex in a pitch-black room either. There's something to not seeing and just touching as well, but not when it comes to getting started on a completely new sexual experience. Save that stuff for a later occasion. Even if a guy is used to completely selfish sex he will take notice if he can see that you want to connect, that you show him how turned on you are. If he's never done it before that way, it's gonna be an even bigger surprise for him, once he discovers how much he's turned on by a woman who so is much into this. If you start with him, make sure you enjoy going down on him (or don't do it, if you're not into it), and make sure he can see that, share your pleasure. If he starts with you...well, then it's easy. If there are things he does in a way that doesn't turn you on, direct him with your hand. If you're not shy, say what you want, but tone makes the music. Not everyone is born for dirty talk. Often it's enough to just say things like "slower," "faster," "more to the right," "more to the left"; whatever it is, you want him to do. And of course say it with a soft voice. But that's really all it takes. You don't need to talk like a porn star.

And then take your time! Make sure you keep looking at each other, make it all about a united experience, not just another hump session. It sounds simple, and it is just that, but it's all about getting really into it. If you have sex for the sake of exploring each other and all that physicality has to offer, you might discover new things about yourself and the person you have sex with. Most importantly, keep an open mind! Take every moment in, let your instinct guide you, stop judging your impulses and be open to let the other person really see you.

When sensuality really takes over, the passion will rise and you can go to places you've never dreamt of. Whether it's more the soft, tender kind of sex or the wild porn star kind of sex, whether it's kinky or more "conservative," all of it will lead to the same thing. Eventually you will melt together with the other person's energy and something incredible will happen. Include all your senses! Again, women are often opposed to the visual because they're taught that sex is all about emotions for a woman.

Therefore, the lust part, the part where you allow yourself to be turned on by looking at your man, penetrating you, how he thrusts deep into you, is often shied away from. Lust, desire, raw animalistic passion is so damn beautiful! You have no idea what you're missing!

ALL MEN love seeing their sex partner melt away in lust, there are NO EXCEPTIONS. In that moment, it's all about primal instincts. If they wouldn't matter, we wouldn't have them in the first place.

We are sexual creatures by nature. But if you never experienced sex as a mind-blowing experience, you obviously won't crave it as much. If you really allow yourself to let lose, to cut adrift, you'll have a very different experience; I can promise you that. Any woman can become a sexual force, and she will, once she had that incredible, mind-blowing orgasm.

Again, this is not about sexual acrobatics (obviously they *can* be part of it, but don't have to), it's about creating a truly passionate experience which allows both to get in sync and to grow into that heavenly explosion... You'll find out how sexual your true nature is. I can guarantee you that.

Now, in casual relationships/hookups the flirtatious part should come naturally since it's a person that doesn't experience you on a regular basis, therefore it's not so much about breaking through established behavior. The downside is that you don't know what they're into. But like everything else, everything has an upside and a downside. Turn the weakness into strength! Just pay attention to each other. See what he responds to; show him how he can please you. Play the game of seduction, give and take, give and take.

I can't repeat it enough: *men love women who love sex.* Women who have had really good sex want it just as much as men. All the women I know who had this kind of sex love it. They might be in a relationship or have casual hookups. It doesn't matter, it's about enjoying the pure physicality of it whether you're in a relationship or not. Sex starts in your head. You can have an incredible experience with a complete stranger, just as much as with someone you know well. The key is the mind. Drop all these pre-conceived ideas of what you are and what you're not. Discover yourself and the other person as if it was for the first time.

If you're drawn to someone, it's an instinctual thing, something that you can't explain with words. If it's there, it's there for a reason.

You can't go wrong with that. Women are often stopped from beliefs that weren't theirs to begin with. "I can't have sex without love," "I can't let go with a stranger," "I don't trust this guy," "I'm not a slut," and whatever else you might have learned growing up and as an adult. Most of the things we have accepted as something we believe in are in fact not really our opinions, but the opinions we were taught by others and a result of social pressures. Stop thinking so much about what others might think of you. You can't control that anyway. Other people's judgment of you has very little to do with your actions, it's based on their beliefs. This is your life, not theirs.

Chapter 11:

PERSONALITY FACTORS

There are some personality traits that will enhance your sex life tremendously:

Confidence:

A scenario:

Guy meets girl: They sit on a table, getting to know each other. On a physical level, they clearly find each other attractive but what really counts will be the difference in the energy between them.

An important observation:

Whatever is in your mind will translate into your vibe!

Let's say she has a bit of an off day and feels self-conscious about her looks. If she sits there doubting herself because she feels she doesn't look her best, it will surface in the way she presents herself. It will change the way in which she participates in the conversation and in her ability to read his body language. Most importantly, she won't be able to be in the moment. Not only will he feel that she's not really with him, but it will *change the way he perceives her.* In turn, she will feel he's not really into her. It will make her nervous and she will act even more awkward. It's amazing how an attitude can literally change the way in which a person perceives you visually! Confident people will smile in a way that you can't help but see the sparkle in their eyes. The sound of their voice, their body language, all of it will draw you in.

Same goes the other way around. You can sit across from one of the most gorgeous hunk's you've ever seen, if he's insecure it will make him way less desirable to you.

I've seen it time and time again. A somewhat pretty girl who has confidence, knows who she is and lets her best side shine through can outdo a true beauty just because of her vibe. If a true beauty has no personality, no energy that will draw a guy in, her looks will wear out fast, whereas her pretty friend with the captivating energy will walk away with the hot guy. There's also the phenomenon that very beautiful women often rely too much on their beauty because they naturally get attention that way when they walk through the door. But, if that's all they have going for them, it won't get them anywhere. I've seen plenty of beautiful women who couldn't hold on to a guy because they simply didn't appear very lively. Obviously, there are true beauties with a great and interesting personality to match; they're just rather the exception than the rule.

That's why there are people only viewed as beautiful while others are considered hot. So what makes one hot? Is it just their body? While that might be part of it, it's never the only thing.

A hot person has an energy that makes you take notice. You want to be around them, feed of it, touch them. There's something about them that makes them irresistible. They have some unexplainable light they shine outward that others simply don't have. It's in the way they talk, smile, move, and look at you. They radiate a certain kind of energy that is so powerful that they can walk into a room and everyone will notice them. It's because they know who they are and it shows.

Try the following next time you got out: Make it easy for yourself by dressing your best. Just look in the mirror and take in all your best traits, whether it's your eyes, your lips, your boobs, your legs, your butt, your hair, whatever you can find on yourself that you find attractive. Then, consider everything that makes you special (your sense of humor, your laugh, your smile, your feisty attitude, your intelligence, your social skills, and whatever else you have) and focus your attention on that. Then, when you're heading to a bar with your girlfriends, walk into the bar very self-aware. Pay close attention to the way you walk, do it slower than usual, be very present. If you find it a struggle, imagine a woman you admire (a movie star, a singer, a female friend who is the way you'd want to be) and pretend you're her for tonight. I can pretty much guarantee you, if you take this to heart, people in the bar will take notice of you.

This is a very good first step. Practice this for a bit on different occasions, the more you practice the better you'll become. If you needed to cheat by imagining being the woman you admire, eventually you will develop a certain confidence, and the make-belief factor will fall away. Then, when some guy approaches you, stay in that mind frame. Don't think of what you did in the past. Just see this as a completely new scenario. This is a different you, one who deserves this attention. Take it in as if you just met a great guy for the first time (any guy). Don't expect anything. Don't try to anticipate what's gonna happen next. Just go with the flow, stay in that open and very present mind frame. Eventually you will get used to the attention and expect it. Once that happens, you're on the right track.

It takes time to break old habits and to develop confidence but anyone can do it. I've seen men and women who were just slightly above average in the looks-department take home the most desired person in the room (or just getting their phone number to meet up some other time). Sure, it helps if you make yourself look your best. It's part of human nature to be attracted to a certain kind of beauty, just the same way you admire a beautiful piece of art. However, when it comes to attraction between two people it's much, much more about your confidence.

To be clear, I don't mean cocky behavior or arrogance! That's actually the opposite of confidence. A cocky guy is in reality usually very insecure. Otherwise, he wouldn't feel the need to prove to the world how cool he is. The same goes for an arrogant woman. Why would you need to make someone else feel smaller in order to feel bigger? A truly confident person won't lose perception of themselves just because there are other people that could be "better" or "lesser" than them. It simply makes no difference to them since they know who they are. They don't feel threatened by others. People put themselves on pedestals because they feel safer behind a shield, in reality they have very fragile egos that can be bruised very easily.

Only insecure people need a mask. Real confidence comes from knowing your qualities (physically and character-wise) and not being afraid to show them. A confident person can have eye contact without fear. They're open to take in whatever comes their way because they know they can handle it. Don't compare yourself to others. There's always someone who might be "better" than you in something so don't worry. You are a package deal. *The sum of you* makes you unique and interesting; never lose sight of that.

Confident people don't make themselves smaller or bigger than they are. They just stay in the moment and allow themselves to just be. That's very attractive. It's hard to do for most people because we're all taught in one way or another that we're not good enough the way we are. Forget what others think. They're not you and they just might have their own agendas for their critique that might not be to your benefit.

The confidence factor is so important when it comes to relationships of all sorts, definitely if you want love, and even if it's "just" about sex.

Sensuality:

I've mentioned that word quite a few times. For all those who don't really know what it means, let's just say you hear a song you like, something upbeat and you start dancing. You can dance mechanically, since you know how the rhythm is but if you really let the beat and the emotion click in, it triggers your body (music always triggers emotions and often memories as well) and if you don't care of who's around you, your motions will be different. You become one with the beat and you will enjoy how it makes you feel. Just follow the flow and your dance will have a completely different vibe.

Another situation is when you sit with someone and you have a conversation. Do you only listen to the words they say or do you really pay attention to the sound of their voice, how they blink their eyes, where they look while they talk, and their body language? Do you notice how their pupils change during the conversation, where they turn their eyes? This is all part of being sensual, using your senses to take the other person in.

When you touch someone, can you feel their response? Do you really feel their skin, the temperature, hairs, and texture? Can you tell how it feels to them? What it does to you?

A sensual person just takes things in much more consciously. It also has something to do with enjoying what we see, hear, feel, smell, and touch. It's like discovering something the first time – over, and over and over again.

That's the key... it's all about paying attention to something or someone as if it were the first time. Be present in the moment!

Chapter 12:

LEAVE THE PAST IN THE PAST

If we could push a reset button, we would do a lot of things differently.

All our actions are colored by our past experiences. While that can be a good thing if they're positive experiences, it often hinders us to truly explore something because our minds compare any new experience with prior similar situations. When an experience is connected with emotions, that habit is amplified but how does that relate to sex?

Simply put, you have certain memories about past sexual experiences that will influence not only how you see yourself sexually (sex drive, how much you enjoy it, what you're willing to do/try) but also how you will approach future sexual encounters.

That can be a problem if you had bad experiences or just plain bad sex.

For instance, if you had a very bad experience in a younger age, let's say someone abused you sexually, it might lead to either what they call promiscuous behavior or a lot of tension.

If you had very selfish lovers, who just worried about their pleasure you probably faked a lot of orgasms.

If you were cheated on, you might think you're not such a good lover.

If you were raised by very religious people, you might have learned that sex is necessary for reproduction but not meant to be for sheer pleasure.

All these things will have an impact on the here and now.

Now, imagine you knew nothing of the past, no influence, no bad horrific experience, no shitty relationships, no insults, no disappointments, no judgments, nothing. Then pretend you knew nothing about social structures and labeling.

Envision meeting someone you're attracted to and they're attracted to you. It's just you and the other person. You would be curious, open to them and very much in the moment, since you wouldn't know or *anticipate* what will come your way. That's kind of the place you need to find in yourself, to open yourself up to a completely new experience and approach, to fully enjoy the ride and to really let go.

In terms of bad experiences; depending on the philosophy and/or point of view, some would call these either just really bad luck, bad circumstances, bad people you keep attracting subconsciously, or you simply allowed someone to mistreat you out of low self-esteem.

Ultimately, it doesn't matter what the reasons are but one thing is for sure: NOT ALL PEOPLE ARE THE SAME.

Even if you've had some bad or even horrible experiences, understand that there are good and bad people on this planet. Not everyone is like the person you encountered.

Obviously, if you had a really bad encounter (rape, abusive violent relationships) you might need some help from a psychologist/therapist. At some point, once you worked through it, you should really try to let it go. It is important to liberate yourself. If a person abuses someone and the abused feels like they will never be able to have a relationship or sex, the abuser wins and continues to have power over them. Work through it and take back your power.

See it as a rebirth, a start-over; take yourself consciously out of the victim state. You're the only one who can take charge of your life. Hopefully – if you had therapy – your therapist was able to make you see that none of this was your fault. Obviously, people heal in their own time frame, and only you will know when you're ready.

For all other cases, bad sex, selfish lovers, mishaps and such, it's kind of the same thing (minus the heavy psychological aspect). Yes, you had unpleasant experiences but that doesn't mean you have to continue having shitty sex.

This is why it's important to decide to start anew. It's not about high expectations, because once we have them, somehow we end up being disappointed. It's because if you play things out in your head, they will always be different than reality. Not necessarily worse than reality, but different and that always throws people off. High expectations also create a lot of pressure. What happens under pressure? People get tense and that's not good for sex! A mind under pressure has restricted airflow and even the arteries tense up. It's gonna take away any spontaneity and playfulness.

Feeling excitement, being open-minded and curious is a different and much better mind frame.

Chapter 13:

PERCEPTIONS

A lot of things, events, relationships, and even sex are related to how we perceive them. Many people are not aware of that. We make all kinds of assumptions about people, what they mean when they talk, what it tells us about them, what they think about us.

It is fairly common that you will hear a completely different description from two people about the same situation almost to a point where it feels like two completely different scenarios just because of the way they interpret what happened. Anything you experience, see, hear, feel or whatever is seen through the coloring of your past. We automatically compare current events to similar situations we experienced in the past. The mind does this automatically. The only way to get out of this, once you're aware it is happening, is to consciously stop yourself from doing it. That's exactly why I wrote earlier that it's extremely valuable if you manage to look at something as if you've never experienced it before. Take on a completely neutral point of view, almost like a child. If you watch a child, you will see that it approaches everything with an open mind. Not because it's dumb, but because everything is new, and therefore there are no other situations to compare a scenario to.

An example:

Two people go on a first date. They don't meet with the intention to hook up, but while they're out a really strong chemistry builds up. They both actually want to go home and rip each other's clothes off, but most likely the female will think that it's gonna ruin a thing that could potentially lead to more while the man will not even think about it. The reason is because society has taught women that there is a format one is supposed to follow, namely to go on a few dates and hold out. Often that takes the fun and lightness away, because she will use all her energy to fight off an urge, while he will try anything to make her give up that resistance. In most cases, she wins that struggle, but is it really a victory?

We frequently give up a lot of our instincts and make a big effort to "do the right thing." But often these choices are more based on mere speculation. No one really knows if things will turn out the way we intend for them to be. In fact, you may never know what exactly is on someone's mind because most hide their true thoughts pretty well.

Yes, there will be guys who will assume that she is an "easy" girl if she sleeps with him on the first date but, truthfully, if a guy is so narrow-minded and judgmental, do you really think that he would make such a good boyfriend? Chances are he will be just as narrow-minded in other areas as well.

So even if you play that "hard to get" game, it won't guarantee that it's gonna work. If he really played a game just to get laid, he will still walk away because he won't make an effort to take you out several times just to get laid. Even if he would take you out several times because he's *that* into you *physically* and eventually you give in, he will likely walk away once he had you if that's all he wanted. Therefore, if anything, you will have wasted your time on a guy who never wanted to get into a relationship in the first place by meeting several times before you end up in bed. And then he will disappear. I personally think that this is much worse.

Think for a minute: The moment you have to play this kind of game to keep someone at bay, doesn't that indicate that they're probably not that interested in you as a person in the first place? And if he isn't, he was still someone you had this great chemistry with, so why not follow your impulse and enjoy a great night together if the chemistry is that strong? If he really likes you, it won't hurt, and if he doesn't, there's nothing you can do about it. You can't make someone fall for you anyway. No one can, neither men nor women.

So, let's get back to the example....the chemistry was there, and if you were to go home with him despite the fact that he might not want to date you, at least you could have a fun encounter with him instead of making such an effort to fight an urge for something your body obviously craved.

I've mentioned this before and I'm gonna repeat it, simply because it's such a stupid misconception:

Either no one is using anyone or – *if we must use a negative term* – *both are using each other for sex.*

I don't know who came up with this weird idea that men are using women for sex, if they were both really into each other. That's just an old, outdated social rule that insinuates that women are still held to some sort of "Virgin Mary" code and that they have to protect their virginity. First of all, most women are not virgins anymore when they ultimately get married, so why make this such a big deal? Second, why save up something so beautiful for that one "special person" who might not turn out to be so special after all? No one really knows this beforehand anyway. I'm aware that I might insult the more religious reader with this statement, but really good sex is truly an incredible gift, to be enjoyed by *both* parties.

In many ways, this notion (that men are using women for sex) was invented to control people, because sex can also be a very powerful weapon.

Chapter 14:

MALE AND FEMALE HABITS

The vast majority of us were taught to take on certain stereotypes while growing up and in turn, we adapted certain habits. Many books on the differences between men and women have been written, but in reality they are not as different as you think. Books like *"Men Are from Mars, Women Are from Venus"* and other similar reads go to great length to explain those differences in nature and behavior attempting to bridge the areas where we supposedly lack understanding each other. Not only is this not true, it misses the point. If you were to raise a boy and a girl differently, if you wouldn't teach them stereotypes such as (just to name a few) "Girls are much more emotional than boys", or "Girls have to be careful because boys will take advantage of them sexually," they most likely would turn out very differently. Both genders would develop their personalities according to their true nature, not according to their gender assigned roles. You wouldn't have adults who can't trust each other, because they believe in the myth of hunters (men) and prey (women).

Besides the obvious physical differences between men and women, I believe it's a cultural thing that made us believe that there is this deep misunderstanding between the genders. When people grow up under these labels, they eventually act the way the stereotype dictates.

We're not born with behavioral patterns, we learn them.

Obviously, men and women are different in certain things, such as looks and physical strength, but when it comes to interacting with each other, I'd rather have my reader judge the other gender by personality than stereotype. Here are a few examples of what I'm talking about:

Female labels:

Women like to talk. Women are always analyzing something. Women can't have sex without love. Women are looking for their mate (for life). Women are emotional. Women are clingy. Women want a commitment. Women are dramatic. Women are irrational.

Male labels:

Men avoid conversations. Men are cheaters. Men are selfish. Men can't show weakness. Men are pigs. Men like to be leaders. Men are simple-minded. Men are superficial. Men are liars. Men think with their dick.

If children learn these kinds of stereotypes, they will likely believe that they're true (because their first role models taught them that) and eventually become adults that identify with gender assigned roles.

Most people never question things they have learned. In fact, they're not even aware that most of their beliefs are *not* based on their personal experiences. It takes a lot of work to figure out what you actually believe and what ultimately may have been forced onto you.

I believe the easiest way to deal with this is to try to be more neutral. What I mean by that is to really observe a situation and/or yourself in it, without these judgments. See how the guy across from you really is. You might be in for a big surprise and find out that he is very sensible, observant or even deep. Fact is that we will never get out of this artificially created communication-mess that is full of prejudice if we don't stop this hideous role-play we've somehow managed to adapt. I know just as many cold, emotionally detached women as I know very emotional, talkative men.

The struggle between the genders is a direct result of artificial misunderstandings, created by social structures. Men and women act a certain way because of what they've learned. If we all would take the time to get to know each other with a fresh and open mind we wouldn't have half the problems we have in terms of understanding each other and that includes relationships and sex.

For the single girl:

The next time you meet a guy don't assume that he has any of these typical "traits." Wait and see what you can observe. Try not to label someone before you know them. I've seen plenty of guys who like to talk, who become clingy, who want kids and a commitment. Same goes for women. Just be yourself. Maybe the real you doesn't want a commitment, likes freedom and fun and is very pragmatic. Maybe not. If he has these pre-conceived ideas about you, that's his problem. You like to talk? Talk! If you're the logical, rational type then be that! Don't try to be a girly girl if you're not. Stay in the moment and figure out who he is by observing.

Relationships sometimes fall apart simply because we're so committed to a role-play (only to find out later that we're not happy with these roles) or we finally get to know the real person (not the role we assigned to them in our heads) and find out that they're not who we thought they were.

Chapter 15:

THE YIN/YANG EFFECT

While this is a book about sex, it won't hurt to address the way people interact with each other because that interaction factors into sexual relationships.

How do people communicate with each other? Any kind of dialogue between two people is always a bit like a dance. If I accuse you of something, most likely you will defend yourself. You may even get angry or feel threatened by me. The more I challenge you, the more intense your defense mode will become.

Simply put, if I force you into a direction you will push against it.

How does this relate to sex or relationships? Remember the women who can get any guy and can turn a player into a man who wants a commitment?

Let's examine what exactly makes a player a player:

Besides the fact that they're usually above average looking and very much into staying in shape, such men likely take great pride in their ability to get any woman in the sack. They get validated through their trophy collection. They're usually very adept in charming women verbally and have excellent observational skills. They pick up on what exactly flatters the female they're trying to pick up and, most importantly, it's more of a sport to them, a game. They love the thrill of the game the same way a poker player does. They are experts in making that particular woman feel special for that specific moment and very few women are immune to flattery. Such men are good at making the rules, leading the game, and they push the woman into a reactive state of mind in which she won't be able to make her own rules. And there you have the key!

Let's say a player meets a woman who is willing to go home with him, but little does he know that she's doing it for the same reason as he does. She just wants to get laid. Let's say the sex is amazing, and they stay at her place. Smart players usually do that because that way they can determine when they leave and they avoid the stalker effect, since she won't know where he lives. But, afterwards, she's the one who's trying to get him to leave, not in a mean, stand-off-ish way, but in a very nonchalant, detached way. I can bet you money that this will throw him off. A player calls the shots. If you turn the tables on him, you have him by the balls, namely his pride.

It's easy for a player to walk away because they make a deliberate choice not to engage emotionally under any circumstances. Now, if he really liked the sex and he finds her attractive, this whole "complementing him out of her house" routine won't fly very well with him. He might be pissed but I can assure you that he will find a way to hook up with her again, trying to break the spell. At first, it might be just for the sake of winning the game, because this has never happened to him before. If he fails again the second time, meaning she will get rid of him again, he will wonder how he lost his magic spell. That by itself is a great starting point to turn the hunter into a prey. If you do that tango dance several times, he'll get used to the sex and hang around more afterwards. Gradually, he can't help himself but notice her other traits (assuming they don't hate each other's personality). From then on they will become steady lovers and, if she stays cool and in control, it will become a bigger challenge for him to try to break her down. If she really likes him, all she needs to do is keep going. Eventually the tables will turn completely. Why? Because it is extremely rare that this happens to a player. He won't understand what's happening and the *last* thing a player wants is to be out-played. If in time he really starts to like her (since he actually gets to know her as a person), guess what? He will be the one wanting to be with her! Subconsciously this has to do with the fact that he sees her as an equal and that he can't have her so easily. She has become somewhat of an enigma to him. He's found his match, his equal. This exemplifies pretty well how a yin/yang/situation plays out.

The same goes for love. Rarely will it ever happen that people love each other equally as strong at the same time. One will always love the other a bit more. Sometimes they may take turns, but it's very, very rare that two people are completely equal in their emotions towards each other at the same time.

Another example:

Here's the story of a girl who has a very free-spirited personality. She doesn't like to cling on someone, she's very independent, not jealous, wants to take things slow when dating and live in the moment. She's also very rational. She rarely feels the need to cuddle after sex (sounds like every man's dream, right?). Considering how men are stereotyped isn't that what they all want, the easygoing type? Most would think that, but what if I told you that most guys she's dated took on the "girl's role" eventually? I'm not talking about girly men, but average men who eventually were the ones who wanted to get her to commit to them in a serious manner. They were the ones who wanted to talk about emotions, and tried to get her to say the three magic words (in case someone is in the dark I am referring to "I love you").

To clarify, the yin/yang effect has nothing to do with gender issues and stereotypes, its plain *human behavior,* and we're all doing it to some degree.

Once one out of two people takes on a certain position, it automatically makes the other person go down the opposite road. In this case, the open-minded chill guy all of a sudden becomes clingy, just because she is not. It is just part of human nature to do that. People can't help but test boundaries, whether they do it consciously or unconsciously. This is why it's downright an art form to balance a relationship between two people.

Some know instinctively when to push and when to pull. A giver often attracts a taker, or turns the other into a taker. For example, if you give in too much (to the other person's will or wishes), the other will take you for granted and, depending on their personality, that will manifest either lightly or much stronger.

Some women have a very good way to keep a guy just enough at bay to have control. She will show him enough feeling to keep him safe, yet not to a point where he will feel too safe and do things to jeopardize the relationship. She will be nice, but she won't allow him to demand anything from her. See it as keeping someone lightly on their toes the whole time.

They say opposites attract. I think opposites are often created.

Chapter 16:

CHEATING

Let's examine the multiple reasons why people cheat a little bit more in-depth:

I mentioned before that it's not in our DNA to be faithful. It might be an inconvenient truth, but it's pretty evident. No matter how in love we are with someone, at some point you'll either see someone you're attracted to on a more superficial or visual level (on the street, at work, on TV) or an attraction will develop while talking to someone and the famous "spark" will grab you. Now, if you really love the person you're with, you will avoid acting on that spark.

If you have a relationship where the sex is exhilarating, chances are it will take a lot to make you cheat. Obviously, it can still happen. The more common reasons are things such as being apart for too long, fighting, insecurity, not feeling validated, and other similar reasons.

If the sex is not so great anymore (or never was), and you have sex less frequently, it tends to make people a bit more agitated or frustrated and that can only add to the feeling of unhappiness. In that case, almost any half-ass opportunity will serve as a good reason to cheat. Even someone less attractive will be a temptation. Actually, that happens quite a lot because when someone cheats with a person less attractive, subconsciously the cheater sees that person as a non-threat to their relationship. They're not looking for someone new to be with permanently. They're looking for someone who makes them feel better sexually, to get an ego boost. They wouldn't break up with their partner for a physically and mentally less attractive one-night-stand.

Another big reason for cheating is sexual preferences, certain things one is into, but afraid to talk about.

A girl who worked in a call center (commonly known as a flirt hotline) talked to many guys as part of her job. Here's what she said: A lot of guys who called where in relationships, telling her that they loved their girlfriend/wife, but were looking for either more excitement in the bedroom or they had sexual desires they were afraid to discuss with their partner. Some others bravely brought it up and got laughed at.

By no means would I want my reader to do something sexually they're really not comfortable with, especially if her man wants something extremely exotic (for instance, being treated like a baby, or eat their feces or whatever else someone could be into). At the same time, if it's something not so exotic (like being handcuffed, having sex in public places, outdoors, wearing a certain outfit, try a toy), I'd definitely recommend to give it a go. Everyone has to find out for themselves what is too much for them. Some might find that they like to be dominated or have a threesome, or watch porn together or do role-plays. I'd say try it out before you reject it, unless you're disgusted by it.

Now, if your partner has exotic desires that you can't fulfill, he may suppress them for a while, but let me assure you that it will become an issue. No one can live against their nature forever. For instance, if someone has a thing for dominating someone, sooner or later they will go out and do that, either with a whore or someone else (in times of internet it's fairly easy to find like-minded people).

Often it's the death for a relationship if two people are sexually incompatible, especially if we're talking about something exotic. Nevertheless, there are still choices and different ways to handle that. For instance, if you deeply love each other in other ways and it's just one particular thing, then you still have the option to allow him to do that with a professional before you break it off. Either way, I think the lack of communicating these kinds of issues are the main cause for this type of cheating. Same goes for people who have a very different sex drive. Couples who have the kind of mind-blowing sex this book is focused on usually don't have this problem (unless they're real sex addicts, and then it's still a matter of defining what too much sex is). For some people it's too much if they have sex 3, 4 times a week, while others love to have sex 3 to 4 times a day.

Another reason for cheating, often handled as a taboo, would be having bisexual tendencies. Bisexuality is much more common than you think. Sometimes those desires are subtle. For example, a man who wants to have her put her finger in his anus or wants to be anally fucked with a dildo, while the ones with a stronger bisexual tendency might need a male body. In that case, you have the choice to either let him have protected sex with a man or you'd have to break it off. Fact is, if he really is into that, cheating will be inevitable since it's something he might be able to resist for a while but not forever. If it's just about some stuff more on the kinky side (like being anally penetrated with a dildo or a strap-on), you might want to give it a try before you decide that's it's not your thing. Here's one way to look at it: Did you ever wonder how it feels to be a man when having sex? Penetrating your man's anus with a strap-on is as close as you can get to that. Sometimes it's all about how we look at a certain thing. I'm not here to encourage or discourage you in terms of what you should or shouldn't try. It's your life and ultimately only you know what you're comfortable with. However, I do encourage you to keep an open mind and consider options.

It's a very personal decision where you want to draw the line. There are definitely reasons why people are bound to cheat or live a double-life. Some women like to close their eyes and pretend not to see it, but I'm not so sure if this is the better choice, rather than facing the issue. In fact, often people make all kinds of excuses to avoid the issues because it would be painful to confront certain truths that would undoubtedly cause emotional pain. Then again, isn't it better to deal with something than live a lie for a long time only to be hurt at the end anyway?

In a milder form, it's the aforementioned lack of communication about what one wants that leads people to cheating. Often, when people try to talk about it and get laughed at or they get scorned, they'll lose the courage to try it again. That's why I'm urging my readers to have an open mind. Maybe you will discover a few things in the exploration process about your own desires that might be less common. In general, if you have desires that you don't live out, there is a big chance that you'll be tempted to cheat. Try to approach the subject with your partner. If you do it playfully, maybe while you're in the foreplay mode, it will feel less like a confession. If you suspect that he has undisclosed desires, find an inviting way to initiate a conversation.

Lack of sex or lack of exciting sex is still the *number one reason* why people cheat. Don't let anyone fool you about that. It has become so common to live in denial that I feel I have to give it to you straight. Yes, there is more to a relationship than sex, but as I already discussed earlier, just because "it isn't a nice thing to say," doesn't change the facts. Sex in a relationship is immensely important. That's why it's a relationship and not just a platonic friendship. Great sex will improve everything; your health, your problems (and your stamina to deal with them), feeling close to each other, and expressing your love for each other regardless of the circumstances.

If someone ends up cheating anyway (for other reasons, like fights, separation for a while), it depends on the relationship if the two can move beyond this. If you can't shake the memory, it will kill the relationship sooner or later because there will be massive trust issues. If the two of you really want to try to stay together, you might need some professional help to work through this but understand that, ultimately, you have to let go of these trust issues and wash the slate clean. I think if both are clear about the reasons why one of you cheated, it's easier to move on, whether it leads to a break up or you stay together.

Chapter 17:

THE MORALITY DILEMMA

There is no way one can write a book about sex without addressing morality, so let's get right to it.

Since our society has laid down the law in terms of what is "normal" and socially acceptable, it has created a lot of issues primarily due to the complexity of human nature. One can argue that it is important to have certain restrictions in order to protect innocent people from getting hurt, but that's about the only thing I can think of. In reality, there are a lot of social rules that have very little to do with protecting people. A lot of these rules are simply made to keep people in check and under control. Often times, they are made to tell people how to live their personal lives. Laws of states and various countries have great variations in how much they interfere with people's personal lives but the vast majority of rules in regards to sexuality stem from religions.

While I'm in no way judging people for their religious beliefs, one must wonder how far any religion is allowed to go in terms of interfering with people's private lives. Spiritual guidance can be a helpful tool in life when it comes to supporting people in rough times, or even in the meaning of life itself, but a lot of these rules are not about spiritual guidance at all. Religion *is* a very big factor when it comes to sexuality.

Why? Because the leaders that made up these rules were very aware of the *power of sexuality.*

As I stated earlier in the book, sexuality is equal to life energy itself. That's why it's so important for religions to make rules about that. For instance, the Catholic Church wants their priests to refrain from having sex, supposedly because spirituality is easier to attain when one is abstinent. Most of us know that, especially in recent years, a lot of catholic priests got themselves into hot water because they were exposed to having sexual relationships to men, women and – much, much worse – children. I believe the reason for that is clear…humans need sex! Just because it's forbidden, it hasn't stopped nature from taking its course. If you need more proof that sexuality is a big part of humanity, this is a perfect example. Let's assume priests do have the best intentions not to engage in any sexual relations at the beginning. Despite all the available guidance, some have not been able to uphold that promise. I'm not suggesting that all have been unable to resist, but many have struggled to do so. As an example, there are countless stories of priests having secret families with their housekeepers. So why even try and torture yourself? It's just not doable to suppress that urge because is entirely natural and an essential part of our nature.

There are also forms of Buddhism where one is supposed to stay away from all earthly pleasures to find enlightenment while others have the rule that it's okay for a man to have multiple wives (Islam, Mormons, and some cults) and yet a woman can't have multiple husbands. I think I don't need to point out the obvious but I will. Such rules were obviously written by men as a way to control women.

So where do we draw the line in terms of interference?

It is clearly important that we have restrictions to prevent people from harming others (sex with children, animals, rape, sexual violence, non-consensual sex) but aside from that, who has the right to tell others what to do in their private bedrooms? As long as no one is forced to participate in something they don't want, it shouldn't be anybody's business. How can any faith that is supposed to be supportive to the individual dictate what you should and shouldn't do including passing judgment on you based on what you're sexually into? It shouldn't matter what someone's preferences are! Whether they're gay, straight, or bisexual, sexual preferences are as wide-ranging as any other human characteristics. People can judge all they want, it doesn't change the facts; you are who you are. It's just the way is and since that is a fact, why can't we just accept that? Why don't we relieve people of that useless guilt that something is wrong with them just because they're not "so vanilla" by nature. I think it's much worse when people feel it's necessary to live out their sexual desires in secret because they're forced into conforming. That's when people get hurt.

There's another situation in regards to morality that has become much rarer but still exists and that is to enter a marriage as a virgin. That alone brings up some really big challenges. Here's a scenario: Let's say you find someone you fall in love with and you develop a really good, emotionally intimate relationship. Since people who are in love want to express their love physically, it's getting harder and harder not to sleep with their partner. Finally, you can't handle it anymore and you decide to get married.

You have this beautiful ceremony, everything goes well, and then you finally spend your first night together. Since you (or both of you) have no experience, most likely it won't be a spectacular night because you don't know your sexual identity yet. It's natural to think that, in time, the sex will get better. But what if you find out that you and your spouse are sexually incompatible? Obviously, as a virgin, you wouldn't have anyone else to compare him to, but here are some clear signs that there may be trouble ahead. You don't like the way he touches you, how he tastes (or vice versa), or there is just no spark at all. While the very first sexual encounter is often awkward for a virgin, once you have sex several times with a person you will begin to get a feel of their sexual energy. In time, you will also find out if you have very different likes and dislikes sexually. Hence, you might be sexually incompatible.

This is the main reason why I think it's a big risk to get married to someone who you don't know intimately. Obviously I'm not saying that you will be incompatible, but there is a big risk that it could be the case. Even if you try to make that work, chances are you'll end up in a divorce, as a relationship is doomed to fail if two people are sexually incompatible.

Here's a thought you might want to consider: Giving up your virginity for the religious minded is all about saving yourself for the right one you pick. So if you found that someone special, wouldn't it be wiser to "test the waters" sexually with them before you get married to them? You could wait for the engagement and then spend some nights together to see if you match. I know that I'm pushing a big boundary here, but it needs to be addressed.

Here's a story of an Indian girl, raised by very religious parents. She found a boyfriend whom she deeply loved. He was not a virgin, but because he fell in love with her, he agreed on waiting. In time that became an issue, since the urge to express himself physically to her had become overwhelming. She wanted the same thing but she mustered up all her strength to resist. Though they clearly loved each other, over time the relationship fell apart because he ended up sleeping with someone else. She couldn't get over the betrayal and a potentially good relationship was ruined. Years later, she still hasn't found her match.

The above is just one example. I could give you more examples of people who got married, never had sex before the marriage, and found out they didn't match and got divorced. It's also an interesting phenomenon that many virgins who got married and eventually divorced became quite the opposite after the divorce by having lots of sex with different people (most likely to make up for missed out experiences).

Now one could argue, what's worse? Finding the right one, getting engaged, and then testing the waters sexually to make sure you are a match or taking that immense risk and ending up being divorced (something deeply religious people don't want either). Alternatively, you could stay in a very unhappy marriage for the rest of your life and that sounds like torture to me.

Another big issue that will likely arise is the cheating temptation in such a situation. At some point, people who've never slept with someone else eventually will wonder how it would be. That's often the reason why high school sweethearts don't stay together and, should you and your spouse hit a crisis, that thought will be even more prominent in both your minds because you're not happy.

There *are* people who will beat the odds, they never had someone else and stayed faithful, but they are a true minority.

Chapter 18:

TRUTH AND FICTION

This chapter will address some of the myths that are out there and whether there's truth to them or not.

Whores - Prostitutes:

Prostitutes are NOT better lovers they just perform a service. They know a lot about people's "dark secrets" but since they don't have sex with customers for pleasure, they will never have great sex with them. It's just a technicality. Some good prostitutes might be able to fake passion, but ultimately it's a job and time is money so don't ever view a whore as competition. If anything, they are the most disillusioned women out there because they've seen and heard it all. They're not better at hooking a man because most of them are emotionally hardened and unable to build a connection with someone they may be attracted to. They have massive trust issues which make it difficult to create any kind of relationship. A prostitute provides a service. Movies like *"Pretty Woman"* tried to sell it as a twisted Cinderella story but fiction does not create reality.

The same goes for porn stars. Just because someone looks hot and can moan on cue doesn't mean they're a sex goddess. They perform on screen. It only looks like real sex. Yes, they stick it in, they suck cock, and it looks good on camera but they rarely have an opportunity to connect with their co-stars. Their lifestyle is definitely not in the same category as incredible sex. It just looks good, and they have few if any inhibitions. In private, they can be just as boring as everybody else or worse, if they "perform" for real life partners the way they do on film. Another myth is that porn stars are nymphomaniacs. While some porn stars do like sex, it's not true for all of them. Sex on camera is nothing but technical. They even have fluffers (people who give the guys hand-jobs or blowjobs off-camera) on set who prep the guys to be ready to go.

Porn:

According to the myth, only men like porn and, if women like porn, it needs to have some kind of storyline around the sex scenes. Not necessarily true. A woman who loves sex and has no partner can enjoy porn just as much as a man. She just needs to find videos with more attractive male participants (unless she's more into women.) A woman who has had mind-blowing sex but lacks a partner at the time can still enjoy porn and pleasure herself watching it. Some women with high libido's can come just as fast as a man watching porn. Yes, most porn is made for guys in mind and that's why we see more women on camera than men. Porn films are made that way so the guy who's watching can replace himself (in his mind) with the mostly invisible male porn actor. He can fantasize to be him. If you could see more of the male porn stars face, it would ruin that element to a certain degree. Fact is that most men watch porn because they're missing something sexually. Either they're not happy with the sex they're having or they're single. Some men are into variety, and, even if they have a great sex partner, they still like to include other visuals. They are the types that often fantasize about orgies as well. If the ordinary guy who likes porn has mind-blowing sex with a partner, porn won't be as interesting anymore.

Here's a little story about the last paragraph. Two lovers have incredible sex, they're both very open-minded, don't mind to try anything and they both like porn individually. One night he discovers her porn stash and he puts a DVD in. They start looking at it while getting it on, but since their sex is so much hotter than what is shown on screen, the porn becomes completely redundant and they both pay no attention to it anymore. If you have discovered out-of-this-world sex, you won't need anything else in that moment.

Nymphomaniacs:

It's interesting that there's only a word for females to describe an "out of control, insatiable appetite for sex" while, at the same time, women are supposed to be the ones that are way less sexual. One reason for that could be, since society has determined that female sexuality is not so much about pleasure, they needed to label the ones who do have pleasure with a negative term. Is there really such thing as a nymphomaniac? Most women labeled with that term could also be called "promiscuous," another negative label. More often these two words are used to describe a woman with an insatiable appetite for sex, often with many different partners, but not necessarily uncontrollable. An uncontrollable sex drive would be a sex addiction (if there really is such a thing).

Sex addiction:

While this term has become fashionable, it's often just used to excuse cheating. Someone couldn't resist and therefore he/she must have a sex addiction. In that case, we should probably clarify what that means. If one truly would have a sex addiction, the urge to fuck would become so strong that they would literally end up going outside and grab anyone off the street to get laid. If we're honest, that is extremely rare. I don't even know if that really exists. I think it's mainly a really good excuse for having cheated, because that way the person who cheated is off the hook. He/she doesn't need to verbalize the real reason why they cheated, because as we all know, an addiction means you can't control it. I'm not saying that because I condemn cheating, I already stated that humans are naturally not equipped to be faithful. However, I believe that it's time that we call something by its real name. Otherwise, we'll never get clarity about human issues, and the confusion will just persist. It takes guts to admit to the real reason why someone cheated, so in many ways blaming a sex addiction is a good way out of an uncomfortable situation.

Promiscuity:

The term "promiscuous" is used two ways. Generally, it refers to women who have sex freely with whomever they want. However, society sees this as a negative behavior, guilt tripping women into believing that it's inappropriate behavior.

The term promiscuous is also used by therapists and doctors to describe a woman who would have sex with random men, not really for pleasure, but for self-punishment. It means she doesn't really want to have sex and does so to devaluate herself. Obviously no one should have sex for reasons of self-degradation. It's a psychological problem that needs to be dealt with.

Men are not called promiscuous. We live in such an advanced society the term shouldn't even be a topic anymore. To put it simply, women can and should not be singled out because they have the same desires as men.

The dominant/submissive relationship:

In almost every relationship, one person is by nature a bit dominant while the other is a bit more on the submissive/passive side. When it comes to sex, there are also those who have a thing for BDSM (Bondage, Discipline, Sadism, and Masochism) where one is the dominant and the other is the submissive.

People not familiar with these practices often confuse this with an abuser and an abused, but that's not really what it is. Psychologically, the dominant person is often the one who doesn't really execute power in his/her daily life while people in power, like executives and the likes, are more into submissive roles. There are many factors that contribute to that role-play but the biggest misconception is the myth that the dominant partner is the one in control. The dominant is the one who's "doing all the work," while the submissive is the receiver, and he/she is the one who sets limits. He will tell the dominant how far he can go. It's always consensual, otherwise it would be abuse.

There are many people who like to include a slight S&M role play in their relationships, such as blindfolding a person, tying them up, slapping them.

Bisexuality:

This might be hard to swallow for some but *everyone* has a bisexual tendency. How strong it is will vary but everybody has it, even if it's to a very small degree. Almost every kid has played the famous doctor games with their little friends, where they check out each other's private parts. Ultimately, a lot of people will favor one gender over the other but there is always the possibility to meet someone who could trigger their curiosity, whether it's the straight person who all of a sudden finds someone from the same gender appealing or the gay person who could be drawn to the opposite sex.

It's not that uncommon that straight people can have an attraction towards the same gender, like straight women who enjoy gay porn, or gay women who like to watch straight porn.

Here's a very good example:

It's the story of a woman who likes to toy with the idea of seducing a lesbian into going home with her.

She was out with a platonic male friend in a club. He told her about his preference for redheads. Since the club was visited mainly by lesbian women, both spotted a very attractive redhead and he verbalized how much he would like to take her home. They made eye contact with the redhead and it became very apparent that she liked the woman much more than the man. The woman noticed that and offered her male friend a bet that she could take her home but he wouldn't be successful if he tried to do so. Shortly after she approached the redhead, they started dancing together. It became very sensual, hot and heavy very quickly. To her surprise she really enjoyed the sexual vibe that was clearly building between them. They pulled each other close and kissed. While this was clearly more the territory of the lesbian, it was the straight girl who became the seductress. They had their hands all over each other and eventually she put her hands under the skirt of the lesbian and reached for her crotch. The lesbian became extremely aroused while being touched through her panties but after a few seconds, the straight girl became more aware of the fact that they were in public and she pulled her hand out. Only moments later, the lesbian's girlfriend showed up unexpectedly and quickly became very jealous. Ultimately, she gave into her girlfriend's desire for the straight woman, and the three eventually sandwiched each other on the dance floor, touching and dancing together. It was all very sensual and erotic. Later, the straight girl realized that they might want to take her home, when one of the lesbians handed her her business card. She thanked them and went back to her male friend who remained standing next to the dance floor in awe.

Now what does that mean? Is this woman really a closet lesbian? No, but she does have bisexual tendencies like most people. She did admit that she felt aroused by the experience but knew, while she was not into vaginas, she did find women occasionally attractive. Since I know her pretty well, I can tell you that she's very much into men and their penises. What does that tell us? Obviously, given the right circumstances and opportunities, a person can be attracted to someone who doesn't fall into their usual gender preference, even if they end up not getting involved with that person. The degree of bisexual tendencies in a person might vary, but it is undoubtedly there. I'm also pretty sure that most of you know girls who French-kissed other girls – maybe even you did – and while they usually claim that they did it for fun, it still takes a minimum level of attraction to follow that impulse, even it's just a game.

I remember the story of a very straight man that hired an escort and found out that she had the traits of what's often called a hermaphrodite (her clitoris is very large, almost resembles the looks of a penis) and he admitted that it turned him on. He, too, is very much into the opposite gender and generally not attracted to men.

For the most part, it's a matter of *being exposed* to a situation to find out who you really are. Does that mean that you have to give in to that impulse? No, but I think it's important to accept it as being part of who you are.

Sexuality is just very complex, just as people are in general. And that's precisely the reason why we have to be less judgmental and open our minds to the idea that people could potentially have a lot of different faces in the bedroom as well. It's simply part of human nature.

Sexual compatibility:

People's sexual desires are as unique as their personality traits. You'd be surprised how many people are way less "vanilla" (meaning ordinary) than you think. The shy guy you meet every day at the office might be the one who's a foot fetishist, or the lady who works at the bank might be into autoerotic asphyxia (a practice where the person has an orgasm while being strangled in some form). You never know what really hides behind someone's façade. You need to consider that when you get into a relationship with someone, there could be a lot of "dark secrets." I use that term with great reluctance because it insinuates that it's something negative. I do so because it's a common phrase for hidden desires but in no way do I mean to berate anyone's sexual preferences. It takes time to reveal certain things to a new partner. Aside from that, many people feel reluctant because they had a negative experience in the past when a partner didn't take their "confession" so well. For a person to come forward with something a bit out of the ordinary, it often takes some guts and maybe a little time to build up enough confidence and trust to do so. When that happens (if your partner is brings it up), it's best to keep an open mind and see if it's something you might want to try out. Most importantly, don't berate them in any form. Oftentimes these desires are not so far "out there," meaning it could be something simple as a guy wanting his lady to wear a certain outfit, spank her, likes it a bit rough, or wants her to do more dirty talk. It goes without saying that it could be the other way around. You want something a bit more unique and you're afraid to say it.

Here is my take on it: It's definitely better to bring it up to find out if you're sexually compatible. There are a lot of things people can try, but sometimes it might be too much of a stretch (for example if someone wants to be seriously hurt while having sex).

The same goes for a very different libido. For the most part, if you have the kind of incredible sex as discussed in this book, that shouldn't be a problem because you're in a sexual paradise but, in some cases, it could still be an issue. Let's say one wants to have sex 4, 5 times a day, while the other can't handle more than two, 3 times a week.

If the sexual preferences are very different and you can't compromise in some form, I can pretty much guarantee you that the relationship will not work out. Unfortunately, people often end up dragging it out, sometimes for years, before the inevitable happens and they part ways.

I knew a couple where the woman was very "mainstream" sexually, while the man was rather exotic. He was into sex with transsexuals and transgender people and had a thing for very young women (he and his girlfriend were middle aged). He loved the BDSM scene, exotic porn, anything out of the ordinary – you name it. While he was a really nice guy and loved her, he was living a double life and had been for years and he knew that she could never deal with his secret. They loved each other very much but by chance (he was in the hospital and she went through his stuff to bring him clothes) she found out about it. Obviously she was deeply hurt, and he felt very embarrassed. Ultimately it resulted in a break up. One can argue if they couldn't have saved years by being more open with each other, and ultimately prevented a lot of pain, as a breakup is always inevitably harder the longer you're together. I think it's never smart to let it come that far, because eventually it will come out, one way or another. The hard truth is that one can't suppress their true nature forever, no matter how much they love their partner.

While there are a lot of things people can try if they keep an open mind to make it work, some things are just not doable. For those who are in such a situation, whether you suspect it with your partner or you're the one who's carrying around a dark secret, try to approach the subject with your partner in a subtle, understanding way. Signal that you're okay with talking about it. Yes, it will take a lot of guts to bring it up, but never forget that your partner loves you. Hopefully, they will react in a way that reflects their love. If not, it just adds to the fact that you're partnership was not meant to be. As long as these conversations are handled with dignity, respect, and love, it should be fine whether you want to try and experiment with whatever the fantasy or preference or not and it's the end of the road for the two of you.

The infamous size issue:

I'm referring to the size of his penis. While most people will claim that it doesn't matter, to a certain degree, it does. If he's one of the roughly estimated five percent of guys who has a real underdeveloped penis, it will be a real issue. Oftentimes it's been said such men are really good in pleasing women simply because they can't make a women come by penetration. If a guy is very big and the woman has a rather small vagina, that will be an issue too. There are positions that can make up for that, so you might need to try a variety of them to see if they help for either case (small or big.) If a guy is really big, it will help if you exhale while he starts penetrating you (at least at the beginning). Exhaling will help you relax the muscle and you'll perceive it as a bit less painful. Do the same when having anal sex. The anal muscle is very strong and if you're afraid, it will tense up even more.

Then there are myths of size in regards to ethnicity or that you can determine what you will get by the size of their hands or noses.... While there are averages, such as black guys have a tendency to be bigger while Asians are on average a bit more on the smaller size, in reality it varies. There are black men with smaller penisses as well as Asian men with a bigger manhood. Interesting enough, no one ever made these assumptions about women's vaginas (let's say that the size of their lips would give you a clue of the size of the *other* lips....) There are guys, rather small in frame, with smaller noses and hands who have huge penisses, just as there are big guys with really small ones.

Indications of a good lover:

The only clue to that would probably be the way he kisses. A man who's clumsy with that will most likely not be the best of lovers. A guy who's a good dancer often indicates to be a good lover as well.

Chapter 19:

THE DO'S AND THE DON'TS....

Threesomes:

Most guys have the fantasy to have a threesome with two women, some even with a guy and a girl (the lesser common version). Obviously, women can have these fantasies as well. While there's nothing wrong with trying/doing that, I highly recommend that you do this with a stranger. DO NOT use his best friend, your best friend, in fact, no one who is part of your social life. I can pretty much guarantee you that it will become an issue, and you could easily lose a friend or, at a minimum, it will become slightly awkward afterwards. While your venture is supposed to be an exploration without emotional attachment there are still egos involved. Even if everyone agrees on the terms and the third party is not in love with either one of the two, it's much more challenging to pull it off. A threesome is supposed to be just for fun, and if you involve a friend, it's someone you will see and deal with after your ménage à trois and there's no way of knowing if it might trigger some unexpected emotions or insecurity from your partner's end or yours or theirs.

If you're single and you have the desire to try a threesome, that's much easier because if you do it with two strangers, there's definitely nothing to worry about afterwards. You can just have fun and walk away.

The same goes for group sex/swinger parties. If you do that with a partner, it's important that you're both really mentally ready for this. Don't abandon your partner once you're there to play! That will only create jealousy and lots of insecurity, even if your partner has a strong self-esteem.

Make up sex:

Men like it, women oftentimes don't. Psychologically this has to do with the fact that women often see sex as a rewarding tool. This is a direct result from the misconception about the gender roles and their sexuality. Hopefully by now you have a slightly different idea of what sex should be. When a couple fights and the energies and frustrations are built up, there comes a point where feelings become so overwhelming that the vibe turns and all of a sudden you want to grab the other person and really give it to them.

Sometimes it can be very helpful to give in to that desire. Giving in has nothing to do with punishment. It's about an extremely bottled up energy that needs to be released. From an instinctual point of view, you're spot on if you feel that urge because sex with that amount of energy will not only be intense it will also turn into one hell of a pressure release. Look at it from a different angle; this is a person you love despite the argument you're having, and often this emotion (love) can turn into a negative where you almost hate your partner. We all know that hate is just a negative expression of love because you hate the other person for what they're not giving you, for not reacting the way you want them to. Ultimately, it means that there is still a lot of love, as the opposite of love would be indifference. Maybe you're just stuck in that anger, and if you give into that desire to have sex in that moment, you'll be reminded of how deep your love for each other still is. Therefore, angry sex can be quite beneficial.

After you're done, it would be the best time to talk about your issues because you'll be able to do so in a much calmer manner, and you'll do it after you're reconnected.

Videotaping sex/sending x-rated text messages:

While it can be a lot of fun to record the two of you having sex, I would definitely recommend that you delete the recording after you've watched it. Trust is all good and well but there's always a chance that this recording ends up in the wrong hands (purposely or by accident). Same goes for x-rated pictures emailed or texted to someone. If you still want to do it, be smart and make sure that no one can identify you (visible tattoos, or much worse, your face!)

Bad bedroom talk:

This is mainly relevant for couples. As mentioned early on in the book, a man who is aroused will almost agree to anything while having sex, therefore it's NEVER wise to have talks (other than dirty talk) while you're at it. Plus, if the sex is truly mind-blowing, you won't be thinking straight anyway, so there shouldn't be any of that going on. Same goes for things people say in the heat of the moment that could be very emotional. DO NOT take that for face value. If there's anything you need to talk about, save that for later, after you're done. The timing for a talk is always good *after* great sex, since you have just connected in the deepest way possible and your emotions are likely not be so mind-controlled. Chances are, you both will be much more honest with each other and you will feel more relaxed.

Another no-no is *specific* sexual details from previous lovers. If only for ego reasons, even a person with a high self-esteem might very well end up comparing himself to the ghosts of the past. Same goes the other way around; you probably wouldn't feel so hot either if you heard specifics about your partner's sexual encounters with a certain ex. More open-minded people likely won't have a problem discussing *what* they've done sexually but it's not wise to reveal *what exactly you did with whom.* Don't give them a face to the story.

Vaginal gymnastics:

Yes, that might sound funny to some of you, but if you ever went to a gym and saw older women naked, you know what I mean. This is definitely not meant to be offensive towards older women. It's just a fact of life. ALL PARTS of our bodies sag with time. We learned that we need to train our bodies in order to keep in shape and the same goes for the vagina. If you want that part of your body to look good as long as possible, do Kegel (pelvic floor) exercises. They're not only good for women who gave birth, every woman should do them! Not only will it make your vagina look good, but it will also keep you tight and prevent a weak bladder when you get older.

Chapter 20:

EMOTIONAL VS. NON-EMOTIONAL SEX

I want to make sure that you understand what I mean when I use the terms "emotional" and "unemotional." Many people commonly associate these terms with feelings of love hence my title for this chapter.

First and foremost, sex brings a strong physical stimulation of the senses whether you experience it in a serious relationship or with a one-night-stand.

Yes, it can happen that we feel something when we hook up with someone, even if we had no intentions of getting emotionally involved. This is probably the hardest thing to break down because human emotions can be very complex. One reason is that we merge our energies in the act of sex (the one of a kind I'm talking about) and we sense the whole being of the other person. It could be something familiar in their vibe (like a kindred spirit connection) that causes your emotions to come up. While there are many theories on what exactly attracts people towards each other, it remains a mystery. Personally, I believe that we are attracted to people when we can relate to the essence of that particular person (also referred to as *really getting someone)*.

The cautious ones among us may fight that feeling, mainly because it's unexpected and you are caught off-guard. Rest assured though, when that happens it's a two way street. There's just no way that just one of you experiences that feeling. Since this doesn't occur a lot, it's probably wise to see if it's something worth pursuing.

Another interesting aspect is the one where the situation is reversed and a person develops feelings of being in love *before* they ever had mind-blowing sex. If that's the case, it's definitely smarter to figure out *first* how the other person feels about you but you need to be very objective with that evaluation. Mind-blowing sex will definitely deepen any real emotions you might already have for someone, therefore it is wise to lay off on a deeper involvement for the time being, especially if you're not sure about their feelings towards you. Any kind of conclusions you draw should be based on *facts*, on what you see. There are always signals that will tell you where he stands. It's hidden in the body language and the way they look at you. Do you see their pupils widen when they talk to you? Do they touch you a lot in a conversation? Is there a big sparkle in their eyes when they look at you? These are all dead giveaways. Obviously you still won't know if that person is ready *to give in* to these emotions, if you came to the *unbiased conclusion* that they must have feelings for you. However, if *both of you* have these emotions beforehand and you take that step and allow that sexual connection to unfold, it could lead to something extraordinary.

Then there are others who seem to constantly "fall" for every person they have sex with. This is usually more of a female problem, albeit not for the reasons you might assume, that women are just much more emotional. I think it's safe to say that you can blame the "social brainwashing" I mentioned earlier on in the book for that. Most women *learned to believe* they can't separate the two (that sex and love must go hand in hand). More often than not, they're not actually falling for that person. It's still that believe that once they "give themselves" to someone, it has to mean something. Most of the time it's just an excuse to rationalize why they just wanted to have unemotional sex. Of course there are emotions while having sex with someone but they don't necessarily have anything to do with *love*. Lust and love are not necessarily the same. You can be totally into someone, but yet you're not in love with them. Another reason is the human ego. It's difficult for some people to accept the thought that they just "gave themselves" to the other person and yet, this person is not completely smitten by them. I know this may sound harsh, but we can't liberate women from all these misconceptions without complete honesty. The next time that happens, try to analyze this in a neutral kind of way (the same way you would evaluate a friends feelings if they were in such a situation).

Great sex is ALWAYS emotional but these emotions are not necessarily feelings of love or, better yet, a feeling of being in love. Love can mean many different things. Commonly the first thing that comes to mind is romantic love, to be IN LOVE, (the butterfly feeling). However, in reality it might just be the kind of love you can feel for a human being for sharing with you who they are, nothing more, nothing less. That doesn't make this emotion any less valuable, but it has nothing to do with being *in love*. If you have truly incredible sex and you merge your energies you get to know a person in their deepest essence and that is obviously emotional. Even if, at the end, you part ways there are many other emotions besides being in love in regards to great sex. You may feel moved, happy, or exhilarated and truly appreciate sharing that special moment with someone.

Chapter 21:

BODY TALK

Our bodies are as unique as our minds. While we all have the same parts, what stimulates every individual can be quite different. However, here are a few things that men in general really like:

Male genitals:

Men love it when women lick (or suck) the area between the penis and the testicles, the scrotum, or the area between the testicles and the anus (the perineum). They also love it if you suck on their balls (how hard or soft might vary). Same goes for the blowjob itself. Guys without foreskin can handle much more aggressive blowjobs than the ones with a foreskin. The foreskin protects the glans (the tip of his penis) and therefore this area is much more sensitive, so go easy on a guy with foreskin. If he's softening up while you're blowing him, it might help to grab his penis on the bottom with your thumb and index finger by forming a ring around it and holding it a bit tight.

Of course, all guys like it if a woman can take his penis all the way in (deep-throat). However, for many women that can provoke a gag-reflex. If that happens to you, try to relax your tongue more and adjust the position of your jaw or the way your body is positioned. Either one of these suggestions may help to make you a bit more comfortable. However, unless he is on the smaller side, you might still find yourself incapable of doing it. Most women can't, it's a very rare skill.

A lot of guys get a kick out of it if you lick or touch their butthole. Sucking on it (if you don't feel repulsed by it) will turn most guys pretty wild. The only guys who might get a bit shell-shocked by this are the more narrow-minded/homophobic types.

Urine:

Many people are repulsed by the idea to be peed on or to drink someone's urine. However, in the Indian culture it's often used as an ailment (topically and orally.) While I'm not suggesting that you should or you shouldn't use it for sexual stimulation, here's an important thing to know if you feel an urge to try. *Drink a lot of water* before getting started. Urine goes through your kidneys and becomes as pure as it gets (unless you're on heavy medication, then I would not recommend playing around with that.) If you drink a lot of water beforehand, it also tastes very neutral. Some men love the experience because when you pee on their penis it feels like a warm shower (hence the term golden shower).

Switching back and forth from vaginal sex to anal sex:

This is a no-no without cleaning up in-between. I don't recommend anal sex without a condom, as there is a lot of bacteria in the rectum. Most importantly, both of you need to clean yourselves up after anal sex! Switching between vaginal and anal sex bares a very high risk for bladder infections for women.

Sperm:

We all know that the texture and taste of sperm can be quite different. As a general rule, if a man hasn't had an ejaculation in a while, the sperm will often be very rubber-like and not as pleasant to swallow. Same goes for not drinking enough water. This difference in texture and taste has a lot to do with what he eats, drinks and how healthy he is. Foods that can help are pineapple (that's very good for the taste of your vagina too, by the way), kiwi, celery and generally raw foods. Sulfur-heavy foods like the broccoli family, meats and nuts can increase the salty taste – not such a good thing, as sperm is often salty by nature anyway. If all this fails, it would be wise if he gets his hormone levels tested. A low level of testosterone can also be the reason for rubbery sperm.

Condoms:

It goes without saying that they're still the number one protection from STD's. One thing he shouldn't do is have sex with you, take a break and go at it again with the SAME condom. There's a big chance that this condom will end up being pushed all the way into you and get stuck there and you will end up with a humiliating trip to the ER to get it removed.

Chapter 22:

EPILOGUE

If I could hand out all my readers who haven't experienced mind-blowing, out-of-this-world, beautiful sex yet a "memory reset button" in the sex-department, I would do it.

Memories often hinder people from experiencing things under a different light, simply because we are so heavily shaped by them. We define our whole being as a sum of our experiences. It is not easy to relearn things as an adult because the older people get the more they're settled in their ways, and they think they know themselves well.

But here's the truth: a truly wise person will never close their eyes on new experiences, new things to learn, to discover, to explore.

Try to awaken that child in you that wants nothing more than to go out and play, just like you did back then.

Sex is the ultimate way to experience another human being from the deepest core. It doesn't matter if it's a chance encounter, an ongoing love affair or a relationship. Every time you share that unique experience with someone, it is special, even if it's only that one night.

There is absolutely no reason or need to put a label on it. This is your life.

You don't owe anyone an explanation but only to yourself. If you really open yourself up to the experience, you'll discover yourself all over again with every single sexual encounter.

The sexual dance has many different facets and all of them have their own beauty. No two encounters will ever be the same. Stay in the moment and take it all in.

Liberate yourself from all the ghosts of the past, the stereotypes and the beliefs that weren't yours in the first place. Discover with joy who you really are.

Every day marks a new beginning.

Let this be the day where you become that woman that every man dreams of, and most importantly, where your dream to experience life and the true beauty of sexuality finally becomes a reality whether in a relationship, a sexual affair or in a beautiful one time encounter.

It's all in your hands now.

www.ingramcontent.com/pod-product-compliance
Lightning Source LLC
LaVergne TN
LVHW021549080426
835510LV00019B/2453